small

beneath

the

sky

(*a prairie memoir*)

———————

LORNA CROZIER

small

beneath

the

sky

GREYSTONE BOOKS

D&M PUBLISHERS INC.

Vancouver/Toronto/Berkeley

Greystone Books
An imprint of D&M Publishers Inc.
2323 Quebec Street, Suite 201
Vancouver BC Canada V5T 4S7
www.greystonebooks.com

Cataloguing data available from Library and Archives Canada
ISBN 978-1-55365-343-1 (cloth)
ISBN 978-1-55365-577-0 (pbk)
ISBN 978-1-926812-27-4 (ebook)

Editing by Barbara Pulling
Jacket and text design by Peter Cocking
Jacket photo illustration by Peter Cocking;
original photos © Momatiuk-Eastcott/CORBIS (sky);
Dave Reede/First Light (landscape)
Printed and bound in Canada by Friesens
Text printed on acid-free, 100% post-consumer paper
Distributed in the U.S. by Publishers Group West

We gratefully acknowledge the financial support of the
Canada Council for the Arts, the British Columbia Arts Council,
the Province of British Columbia through the Book Publishing
Tax Credit and the Government of Canada through the
Canada Book Fund for our publishing activities.

For Barry and Linda Crozier

and for Lynda H.

And the land around us green and happy,

waiting as you wait for a killer to spring,

a full-sized blur,

waiting like a tree in southern Saskatchewan,

remarked on, lonely and famous as a saint.

JOHN NEWLOVE, *The Green Plain*

small

beneath

the

sky

IN WRITING THIS BOOK, I am indebted to Aristotle, who hypothesized that there must be something beyond the chain of cause and effect, something that started it all. He called this immovable force the first cause.

first cause: light

YOU DON'T KNOW what light feels or how its thinking goes. You do know this is where it's most at home. On the plains where you were born, there are no mountains to turn it back, no forest for it to shoulder through. A solitary tree marks its comings and goings like a pole sunk in the shore of the ocean to measure the tides. Here, light seems like another form of water, as clear but thinner, and it cannot be contained. When you touch it, it resists a little and leaves something like dampness on your skin. You feel it the way you feel a dog's tongue lick your cheek in the early morning. After an hour or two of walking, you are soaked in brightness. When you shake your head and shoulders, you see the spray. If you stay too long in the open, you could drown, its currents carrying you to its source, your body bobbing, then going under, your lungs full of lustre. Nowhere else in your travels will you see light so palpable and fierce. It is too huge for dreams, too persistent for solitude. All day long it touches you with the smallest of its million watery wings.

first cause: dust

IN SUCH clarity of light there has to be its opposite.
Something that smears, stains, drops a shroud and forms
a film across the eye. When the wind is up, the season dry,
the world turns upside down: the sky becomes the earth,
particular and grey, and you breathe it in. You can get lost
in dust as in a blizzard. You need a rope to make it from the
house to the barn and back again. Dust settles on dugouts
and sloughs, on drifts of snow, on the yellow of canola, on
the siding of houses, on washing hung on the line. It rises
in small asthmatic clouds as your feet hit the ground. It
insinuates itself under the thickest hair, forms a thin cap
that hugs your skull, a caul for the dying. It thickens your
spit, it tucks between your fingers and toes, it sifts through
the shell of an egg. Here's dust in your eye and ashes
to ashes. It is the bride's veil and the widow's, the skin
between this world and the next. It is the smell you love
most, the one that means home to you, dust on the grass
as it meets the first drops of summer rain.

first cause: wind

WHAT LOVES the wind in this spare land? Of the trees it
is the aspens, their leaves long-stemmed so they flutter in
the slightest breeze. If you were led blindfolded to a grove
of them, you'd step back, sure you stood on the brink of
Niagara. The mist the wind sprays is gritty on your cheeks,
but it doesn't dull these leaves. Wind flips them and wins
the toss; it frisks them from stem to tip and shakes them
insensible. When they soar, then fall, the leaves forget they
cannot rise again.

Of the unwanted, it is the tumbleweeds, cursèd, straw-
coloured candelabras of brittle stems and thorns. Shallowly
rooted, they leave their rainless gardens of neglect and
somersault like ribs of acrobats across the fallow fields. At
lines of barbed wire stretching from post to post, with
the surety of stone, they build a border, a wailing wall, the
wind hauling sifts of clay and packing them in, so the wind
itself cannot pass through.

Of the grasses, it is the wheat. At dusk, the golden heads
ripe with seeds nod and dream they are that ancient glacial
ocean, swelling and breaking, moon-pulled: you feel an
undertow at the edges of the fields and want to go under.
Seagulls drift above you, forever it seems, as if they'd been

sent from the ark, and they're riding hunger and belief on currents of air. It's easy to imagine you could push off in a boat, wind at your back, going home by a sea that tosses and heaves, without a light to guide you.

Of the animals, it is the badger and the wolverine. They have met their match. They bare their teeth and the wind does not weaken or retreat. They dig in the earth and the wind dives in ahead of them. They bite and won't let go, but the wind can hang on longer. They know wind is the better hunter though they've never seen what it catches, what makes it thrive.

Of the human, it is a woman, though most of her kind hate it, will tell you how it drives them crazy on the farms. This one walks right into it, head lowered, thighs and calves working hard as if she's climbing, pushing the boulder of the wind with her shoulders and chest. There's an energy that gusts inside her; wind steals her soul, adds distance and desire, then gives it back. One woman bent into it, a flat country's Sisyphus, the wind rising. What lungs are capable of punching out such an exhalation, inexhaustible and lowly, blowing farther than any prairie eye can see?

common birds
of canada

THE MORNING sun hammered the roofs of the stores along Central Avenue. I could smell the tar in the black-top, and my skin burned as if I stood too close to a stove with a roast in the oven. In spite of the heat, the two RCMP officers who led the Dominion Day parade wore their dress regalia, tan stetsons, black breeches and red serge jackets with tight collars that grazed their chins. The glare on their brass buttons made me blink.

Behind the Mounties on their regulation black mares rode a posse of local politicians and businessmen. They were decked out in cowboy boots and cowboy hats, some sitting as comfortably as Gene Autry about to burst into song, others slippery in the saddle, reins gripped so hard you could see their hands turning white. If we got lucky, this year's cavalcade would include a hockey player who'd gone on from the Swift Current Indians to an NHL farm camp. He'd be waving from a red convertible with a big Ham Motors banner covering each side.

Some distance behind the riders, so that the horses wouldn't spook, lumbered a life-sized black-and-white pinto made of steel. He clanked stiff-kneed between the float carrying the Ladies of the Nile and the flatbed truck

moving. For the parade and the rodeo we'd go to later, I always wore my red felt cowboy hat with the wooden toggle that made the rope short enough to snug under my chin.

Tommy Ham, the father of my best friend, Lynda, owned the Chrysler dealership in town. I looked forward to waving at him as he trotted by on his big palomino. When he spotted me and my parents, I hoped he'd doff his white cowboy hat and sweep it high above his head. For the first few years, I couldn't understand why my father wasn't on a horse alongside him. After all, when my dad was a kid, he'd raced a gelding named Tony in all the local fairs and won cash prizes he'd taken home to his father. I was impressed when he told me he got to keep some of the money for himself.

DURING THE WEEK, my father drove a green, snub-nosed oil delivery truck with the words *Emerson Crozier* painted in white letters on the driver's door. The Pioneer Co-op paid him a wage to fill the tanks for the growing number of residents who had switched from coal to oil. We were the only family on our block who rented; our neighbours owned their houses. I wasn't sure what that meant, but I knew the distinction was important, especially to my mother, though she fancied up the inside of our house as best she could. Three pictures hung on the walls of our living room. Two were copper bas-reliefs Dad had won curling. One depicted a parrot in a palm tree and the other a covered wagon pulled by horses. The third picture, of a deer beside a lake with a mountain backdrop, was frameless, painted on a piece of particleboard by a man who'd crossed the prairies in the early 1940s and set up his easel in the streets. Dad had bought it for two dollars outside the bar at the York Hotel.

The kids my age in the neighbourhood, including Lynda, went to kindergarten in the mornings. I didn't. In those days, you had to pay for it. My other best friend, Ona, who lived next door, was one year younger. Maybe because she and I still hung around together in the mornings, the absence of my other playmates didn't bother me much. The difference between us didn't show up until the first week of Miss Bee's grade 1 class at Central School. They could read the words our teacher wrote on the board and say them out loud. I could not.

I hadn't known I had a shortcoming in the area of books and letters. Along with a few pocket books with yellowed pages and the black Bible my mom received from the Anglican church when she first took communion, there were three hardcovers in the house—an ancient *Book of Knowledge,* its pages as durable and thick as the cardboard inside a newly purchased shirt; Sir Walter Scott's *The Bride of Lammermoor,* its corners chewed by mice; and the spine and covers, back and front, of Zane Grey's *The Code of the West.* No one ever said what had happened to the rest of the book. The family library fit easily into a wooden apple crate turned to stand on end in the front hall. Inside it, Dad had nailed a shelf. The bottom level and three cardboard boxes along the wall were heaped with comic books. My brother, Barry, had the best collection of any of his friends. At the end of each month, he spent all his newspaper delivery earnings at Bill Chew's on Central Avenue. It was every kid's dream of a corner store, stocked to the ceiling with racks of pocket books, magazines and comics. On the glass counter sat big-bellied jars of caramel milk bottles and hard globes of gum, strawberries with marshmallow centres and licorice cigars that blackened your teeth and tongue.

On Saturday mornings my brother's friends traded comics in our front hall. For that hour or two, the wide passageway filled with the smell of grubby eleven-year-old boys who'd come in from playing Dinky Toys in the dirt, bubblegum wadded in their cheeks like chewing tobacco. Their sales pitches and chatter were punctuated by pauses and pops as the bubbles expanded, then burst, a transparent pink skin covering their mouths and chins. As long as I was quiet, my brother let me watch as he and his buddies spread their treasures in front of them, the titles blaring from the boldly coloured covers. The best bargainer of them all, Barry would get three comics for every one he gave away.

Although he was seven years older and loved to tease, calling me "Turkey Dirt" in front of his haggling friends because of the freckles that dotted my face, my brother never denied me access to his stash of comics. Everything was there, from Superman and Archie to the Classics, which retold the great novels and myths on cheap paper in comic-book style. In those vibrant pages my poetry education began. Evident even to the youngest purveyor was the value of the succinct, densely packed narratives charged with words like POW! SHEBANG! BAM! When my brother shouted them out and pointed to them on the page, they detonated like the circles on the red narrow scroll I stole from him and pounded on the sidewalk with a stone; I dared not borrow his cap gun, even for the shortest time. The stories unrolled so effortlessly in sounds and pictures, I didn't miss not knowing the meaning of the other words on the page.

After the first few days of observing her new students, Miss Bee divided our class into four groups of readers: bluebirds, meadowlarks, sparrows and crows. I was placed in the last group, and Lynda became a bluebird. It didn't take a genius to figure out the difference. Bluebirds were so special that farmers like my uncles and grandfather built houses for them, nailing the small boxes to the fence posts along the fields. When a bluebird took flight, you'd have sworn a scrap of sky had grown wings, and they and the yellow-throated meadowlarks sang so beautifully it was as if someone had tossed a dipper of well water into the air, each drop a clear, bright sound. Even tough men like my dad and grandfather had to stop in their tracks to listen. Crows couldn't carry a tune. They cawed and cawed; something stuck in their throats, and they had to cough it up. They flapped through the air like tar shingles torn loose by the wind. On the ground they walked stiffly, as if they'd had polio like Jimmy Coglin up the street and their legs were caged in metal braces. If too many of them gathered in town, the city sent out a man to shoot them.

Sitting with a group of crows in the classroom, stumbling over the words in our reader, was not where I wanted to be. I felt no anger at Miss Bee for her lack of subtlety, only disappointment in myself for being stupid. From my desk, I stared at the letters of the alphabet. Along the top of the blackboard, they marched in a row from A to Z, as unstoppable and unreadable as a line of warrior ants.

Every morning, after we'd settled into our desks, Miss Bee walked down the aisles to check our palms and fingernails. On the bulletin board near the door she'd tacked two big hands. One was cut from white bristleboard, the other from black. If you passed her cleanliness test, she pinned your name, printed on a strip of paper, on the white hand. If you failed, she pinned your name on the black hand, and often that happened to me. Dirt loved my fingernails; it wormed under them even if I'd cleaned them on the way to school with a toothpick. Some of my classmates never got to move from the black hand to the white, and I felt sorry for them. They were the kids who didn't have the right kind of scribbler and whose crayons had worn down to nubs they could barely hold.

A few months into grade 1, I walked home after school with some new friends who lived a couple of blocks from my street. At the top of our alley, one of the girls pointed out my house, with its ramshackle garage, buckled back porch and junk-filled yard. "I wonder what poor people live there," she said.

"Maybe it's the Thistledownes," the other girl replied.

The Thistledownes were known to be on welfare. I'd seen the shack they lived in near the swimming pool. The six Thistledowne kids came to school in old clothes that never fit, and they smelled bad, but once a week they spent money on candy. That I could never understand. We weren't on welfare, we weren't *that* hard up, yet Mom rarely gave me money for sweets.

I walked half a block farther with my new friends. Then, I ducked down the nearest alley and snuck back home.

OUR TWO-STOREY house with its wide front verandah, now collapsed, must have been beautiful years before the landlady had let it run down and my family moved in. My parents didn't have the wherewithal or the money to repair what was broken or to clean up the yard. Ona's house was the same vintage and style, but the flash of its clean white paint made you wish for sunglasses, and the house front yard displayed to passersby a bed of rose bushes and a neat, trimmed lawn bisected by a cement sidewalk. Three doors down, Lynda's house was the newest on the block. Their small stuccoed bungalow had been built by her father. When he was in a good mood, sitting in his favourite arm-chair with a drink beside him, Mr. Ham would talk to me and Lynda in the voice of Daffy Duck. On the doors inside their house shone glass doorknobs like gigantic, multi-faceted diamonds, and on the living room wall hung the only piece of real art I'd ever seen, an oil painting of the cutbanks south of the city limits done by a local high school teacher named Mr. Uglum. My mom was not impressed. She couldn't understand why anyone would want a picture of something they could see every day just by driving five minutes to the edge of town.

Lynda took singing lessons, and she and Ona studied dancing and piano. Lynda showed me how to shuffle-off-to-Buffalo after her first few dance classes and how to play "Chopsticks" with two fingers on the keyboard of the piano that sat glossy and square-shouldered by their big green couch. Ona's piano was in a room off the kitchen that her mother called the parlour. From our backyard, I could hear Ona practising every Saturday morning it was warm enough for the windows to be open, the sounds of her finger-work drifting through the screens. Sometimes I climbed to the top of one of the oil drums Dad had hauled home for salvage and did a little dance by pounding my feet in time to the song she was playing over and over, waving my arms about the way I thought a ballerina would. I felt envious of Ona, but then she was the one cooped up inside on a weekend morning.

To move up the bird ladder at school, I threw myself into the thin books I was allowed to take home from the six shelves in the grade 1 cloakroom. I asked my mother to help me unlock the secret code that filled the pages. So I'd feel better, she joked that maybe I was a crow because of our last name. My brother had been nicknamed "Crow" for a while, until he grew tired of it and threatened to punch anyone who called him that. After finishing the supper dishes, Mom would sit me on the couch and help me read out loud, making me stop and go back to the start of the sentence if I didn't get the sounds right. I knew she hadn't had any books to read when she was a child; she had no favourites among the collection I brought home, and she didn't get bored. The stories were as new to her as they were to me.

It didn't take me long to fly from where the crows gathered to the more ethereal habitat of the meadowlarks and then the bluebirds. At home, Mom and I were soon into the old *Book of Knowledge* my brother had gone through several years before. Some of the pages were water-stained or marred with black crayon that I'd stroked across the paper as a little kid. Mom and I went over and over the page called "Little Verses for Very Little People." I memorized "Rub-a-Dub-Dub": "Three men in a tub; The butcher, the baker,/ The candlestick maker;/And they all jumped out of a rotten potato." The last line never failed to make us laugh. Many of the stories in the book were beyond me, and Mom, too. They sounded like nothing we'd ever heard before, but I delighted in the strange phrasing. If I was playing by myself outside, I'd recite into the lilac branches the first sentence of "Common Land Birds of Canada": "The Orioles and the Meadowlarks are relatives of the Blackbirds, but differ markedly in their habitats."

One spring day Miss Bee led me and another classmate down the hall with its dark oak floor and wainscotting to the grade 2 classroom. Standing in front of the teacher's desk, each of us in turn read a page of the grade 2 reader without having seen it before. I got stuck on the word "detour" and tried to slur over it, but Mrs. Anderson, the other teacher, stopped me. "A good reader doesn't skip over words," she admonished. I felt ashamed for trying to fake it, but the older students clapped anyway when I was through.

At the end of the year, Miss Bee awarded me the prize for having read the most books in first grade. It was a black plaster-of-Paris cocker spaniel leaning on its front elbows, bum in the air, as if it were about to pounce. When I brought the prize home, Mom put it on the china cabinet beside my brother's first hockey trophy. Eventually, the spaniel ended up on my bedroom dresser. Its head tilted like the RCA Victor dog's, but it wasn't music from a phonograph its long, curly ears were waiting for. Alone in my room I read out loud, as I had once with my mother, passages from the old *Book of Knowledge:* entrancing descriptions and perfectly punctuated sentences that might have flowed from the pen of an English governess. Over and over I recited the verses I had to memorize for school, and, later, the mantra of a boy's name married to every rhyme I knew. My plaster spaniel sat loyal, attentive, listening.

by and by

ONE AFTERNOON when I was four, my father came into our kitchen with a toy Pomeranian tucked into his jacket pocket. Unbeknown to his boss, he had traded a half tank of oil from his delivery truck for one of Mrs. Rittinger's purebred pups. Red and furry, the dog was smaller than my father's hand. Lying on my belly on linoleum warmed by the fire in the wood stove, I watched her small pink tongue lapping milk. The thread of white stretching from the surface to her mouth didn't break until she'd licked the bowl clean.

My mother named her Tiny, and she became my brother's dog. The seven years between us made me more of a nuisance than a playmate, but sometimes Barry would let me tag along when he and his friends played kick the can or built a soldiers' fort out of the log ends waiting to be chopped for the stove. As soon as he grabbed his jacket from the hook, I was at his heels like a second dog, dumber in canine ways but just as loyal and underfoot. Some days he'd order me to stay in our yard. Other days, by the caragana hedge, he'd tell me to hide and he'd count to ten, and then he'd never find me. Tiny wasn't sent away unless the games spread too far afield. "Go home, Tiny," he'd say, and she'd wend slowly down the block, head and tail lowered. I knew exactly how she felt.

On winter mornings from the picture window, I'd watch Tiny and my brother head off on his paper route, her trotting ahead, running up the steps to the houses that took the news and passing those that didn't. Our neighbours thought this was the smartest, cutest thing and tipped my brother with change left over from the milkman. Once I went off with them because Mom was curling in a bonspiel out of town and had left the house early to make the first game. All down the block, every house or so, Tiny leaped straight up, as if springs had been buckled to the bottom of her paws, so that she could see above the snow piled on both sides of the shovelled walk. When my brother's bag was almost empty, he lifted me and set me inside on top of the papers he had left, Tiny bounding ahead on her short legs and doubling back. I was so proud and happy. If he'd told Tiny any time, "Go home," she'd have known exactly where to go, but she didn't have to. The three of us had work to do, lights coming on one by one in the windows down the winter streets, the snow blue as flax just before the dawn.

Because my brother tossed so much in bed, Tiny slept with me. A cranky little dog, she'd bite if I moved my feet. I learned to lie like a courtly lady on a tomb, dog on a carnelian cushion at my feet. No one would have guessed in the morning I'd lain all night in that neat bed.

MOST SUNDAYS in the summer, we drove to Grandma and Grandpa Ford's farm thirty miles from Swift Current. The farmyard hadn't changed much since Mom was a kid. The barn sagged in the middle, but the house looked exactly the same. It had only two bedrooms, and she and her six siblings had slept in one bed. There wouldn't have been room for a dog on top of the blankets, even one as small as Tiny. We must have all stunk to high heaven, Mom said, one bath a week in the same bathwater, and sleeping so close. Nobody seemed to notice, she told me. At least they didn't complain.

Uncle Lynton, my mother's youngest brother, had never left home. He, Auntie May Jean and their four children lived with my grandparents in the house's small rooms. As if the place had a magic capacity, its walls seemed to expand when the whole family gathered. For special Sunday dinners, like Grandma's birthday, it could hold nineteen. Though the farm dogs couldn't get past the porch, Tiny was allowed inside. Even my grandfather put up with her as she begged at the kitchen table. But his tolerance had its limits. One afternoon, near the barn, she did the unspeakable: she killed a chicken. Grandpa went to get his gun; Barry scooped up Tiny, ran to the car with her and locked the door. It was an unarguable law in the country: a chicken-killing dog got shot. There was no second chance. Once dogs acquired a taste for blood, no one could stop them.

Mom signalled for me to go to the car with my brother. She told Grandpa she'd pay for the chicken, but he was having none of that. This kind of outrage couldn't be corrected so easily. Cutting our visit short, not even staying for supper, we drove back to town, Tiny in Barry's lap, none of us saying anything about what had happened. For the next several weeks, we didn't visit my grandparents. We waited till Grandma said Grandpa had cooled off. When we went back, never again in his graces but at least allowed to set foot on the farm, we had to leave Tiny behind. That wasn't so bad, because Barry was bored with his country cousins by then and preferred to stay at home on Sundays to hang around with his friends. Tiny wouldn't be lonely, I knew, because whatever they were doing, my brother would take her with him.

That summer Dad won two ducklings at the July 1 fair. He was always good at things like that, playing darts or throwing a ball into a basket. Once he won a guinea pig named Elvis; another time, a one-winged turkey plucked and gutted and ready to roast. Inside the house, the ducklings imprinted on my brother, tagged along behind him across the linoleum when he moved from the table to the couch or walked down the hall to go upstairs. They couldn't climb the steps but fell over backwards and made pathetic quacks. To give Mom a break when they started to get on her nerves, splatting here and there across the floor, Dad banged together a wooden cage and set it near the woodpile outside by the porch. The cage was square, the size of a portable television, with a wire screen covering an opening Dad had cut into the side to let in air. The door, just big enough for me to stick my head through, was latched by turning a flat wooden stick with a nail pounded in the centre.

The yard of our neighbour to the north was built on a slight rise. I played in their sandbox—filled with dirt, not sand—with Dennis, the boy who lived there. He'd just moved in, and I was the only kid who'd play with him, because every day so far he'd worn nothing but a bathing suit. We were building roads for his Dinky Toys: I knew he'd be okay as soon as the other kids saw his collection. He had matchbox trucks, too; how I loved the little boxes they came in. They'd have made a perfect home for beetles, or a daddy long-legs if I could get it to bend its knees.

Dennis was loading a truck with gravel while I pushed a toy Caterpillar with a wide rubber band around each wheel through the dirt, making a machine-like noise in the back of my throat. When I glanced up, I saw Tiny trot across our yard below to the wooden cage. She bit the latch, turned it, and went inside. I could hear the ducklings' squawks and see the cage shift, but there was nothing I could do. It was as if I were in a game of frozen-tag and had to stay locked in the position I was in when I'd been caught. Less than a minute later, Tiny backed out, her muzzle and bib stained red. She turned the latch again, this time to lock the door—she was that smart—then skulked away.

Mom said later that Tiny had been jealous. The ducks had made too much of my brother. I couldn't stop thinking of Grandpa's rage. I thanked my lucky stars, as Grandma would say, that he hadn't been here to see what Tiny had done. I knew without asking Mom that I wasn't to tell any of the relatives. I didn't love Tiny any less after that, but I looked at her differently. I understood why my friend Lynda kept her distance—sometimes Tiny would growl and snap at her when she came near.

FOR OUR GRADE 1 Christmas party, which our mothers attended, Lynda and I memorized "The Gingham Dog and the Calico Cat." With appropriate barks and meows to illustrate their terrible spat, we recited it from the front of the room beside the teacher's desk. Full of the music of rhymes and repetitions, over the holidays I wrote my own poem, about Tiny. She had caused me endless hours of suffering because she often fell ill. Having grown up on farms, both my parents were used to feeding scraps to dogs, including chicken bones. In a creature as small as Tiny, the bones split into shards that tore through her digestive and intestinal system. Every week, the morning after Sunday supper, Tiny dragged her bum around the house and whimpered. Sometimes there'd be a red smear on the floor behind her.

Sure her sickness would be fatal, I had a ritual spot at the top of the stairs on the second-floor landing, where I'd fall on my knees and promise God anything if he'd save her—I'd give up Double Bubble, I'd do the dishes, I'd stop wishing for nicer things. Maybe it was the high drama of my grief and my worry over my broken promises that gave me the idea for my poem—I wrote that Tiny had died. The poem was full of pathos and sadness, with hope shining through in the refrain that I repeated to myself after the Christmas break on the way back to school: "And we shall meet in heaven, by and by." It was like a line from a skipping song.

I was so pleased with the poem that I'd printed it with a fountain pen on a clean piece of paper, and Mom suggested I take it to Miss Bee. Not only did my teacher post it on the bulletin board, but she asked me to recite it for the class. And at recess, rather than sending me outside to play with the other kids, she took me to the principal's office, where I read the poem to Mr. Lewis. He was a tall, formidable man, but we'd seen another side of him when he'd performed in front of the whole school in the gym at the last assembly before the Christmas holidays. On a chair, alone on the stage, he mimed eating popcorn at a movie. You could tell when the action was exciting because he ate his popcorn faster and faster, finally slapping himself in his moustached mouth and knocking himself off the chair. It was one of the funniest things any of us had ever seen, especially because Mr. Lewis's dignified, no-nonsense demeanour usually scared us, whether we were six or fourteen, into our best behaviour.

Everyone believed my tale about Tiny's death and showered me with pity and concern. I didn't want to admit the poem was a lie, so I humbly thanked them for their sympathy. Lynda, who knew the real story, kept quiet. Maybe she thought if I read the poem often enough the mean little dog who nipped at her heels really would fall over dead. By and by, we'd meet Tiny above the clouds, where angelic dogs lay down with ducks and chickens and never growled or bit.

the drunken
horse

O N BOTH sides of my family there was a penchant for drink and horses. My Welsh maternal grandfather brought the two together. Grandpa Ford's father was a wagoner, working on an estate just north of the border near the town of Shrewsbury, where, my grandmother said, the church was round so the devil couldn't corner you. From the time he walked straight-backed out of school in grade 4 because the teacher wrongly accused him of cheating, my grandfather worked every day beside his father, taking care of the horses and driving wagons back and forth from the fields to town. He was allowed to ride one of the draft horses if he wanted to go off on his own after the farm work was done. The gelding he chose was a Shire named Billy, seventeen hands high and an uncommon grey with white feathered fetlocks above hooves that spread wide as platters on the ploughed fields.

When Grandpa reached drinking age, he and Billy made nightly trips to the local pubs. Luckily for him, my grandfather was a singer, and inside, at a table near the window, he bartered a song for his first pint. Perhaps he wasn't melodious enough to get a second or a third sent his way. Those were provided by Billy. It worked like this: my grandfather didn't allow himself to down his first beer. He had to have faith, like the thirsty man who primes the pump by pouring a ready bucket of water down the top, believing the sacrifice will pay off in a fresh stream gushing from the spout. When Grandpa raised his pint, Billy, tied up outside, would poke his head through the open window and guzzle the beer, his master feigning surprise and outrage. The patrons were so delighted they kept the drinks coming for the man and the horse until closing time, when the two would stumble home in the dark. Grandpa said he didn't know who was the shakier on his legs. Some nights he thought he'd have to carry Billy on his back.

The story of the drunken horse sat side by side with my mother's tales of her father's strictness and pride, his meanness to her and her six siblings on their Saskatchewan farm. Mom and five of the other children were born in Canada. Two, including a boy who died when he was six and my Auntie Glad, who would be a trouble to my mother all their lives, had been born in Wales before the family emigrated in 1913. Grandpa didn't say much in later years about the adjustment to a new country, except to call the immigration recruitment officers lying bastards. By the time he arrived in the West, there was no free land left to homestead. For twelve years, he worked as a hired hand and laboured on the railroad until he could purchase a section in southwest Saskatchewan from an American land speculator. Grandpa was allowed to spread the cost over several years by making a payment, with interest, after every harvest.

forkfuls of dry grass. The qualities the Shire draft horse was bred for—endurance and willingness to work—were also his.

Bitterness intact, my grandfather pounded home to anyone who'd listen his hatred for school and teachers, told me to pinch a dog's ear to make it obey, to hit a horse if it didn't behave, and to down a healthy dose of castor oil to clean a body out in spring. His shenanigan with Billy was the only complete story I heard him tell. It showed a warmth he rarely revealed, a sweet affection for a creature that was more to him than just a beast that pulled a plough or wagon.

When I asked my mother why I so seldom saw my grandfather smile, she paused, then said, "Maybe we're each given a certain amount of pleasure we can take from life." The measure the blessèd receive is enough to fill a water tower. In my grandfather's case, his limit was a dipperful. Picturing Grandpa and his horse, the two of them weaving their way down that narrow country road under stars unwashed by city lights, I imagined them come safely to their rest in the barn's close scent of hay and horses, a rest companionable, bone-deep and brief.

milk leg

GRANDMOTHER CROZIER lived in the smallest house I'd ever seen. At age seventy, she'd moved from the farm into the town of Success, just ten minutes away. Her house was like something from a fairy tale that ended badly, but it was a blessing of sorts, because she had trouble getting around. One of her legs, the right one, was swollen to two or three times its normal size. Milk leg, my mother called it, and I savoured those words like a dirty secret from the schoolyard: *milk leg.* I tried not to stare. I imagined her lisle stocking full of thick, creamy liquid, sloshing when she walked like the cow's milk in the tin pail she used to carry to the house from the barn, the cats with their ears and tails clipped by frost following behind.

We didn't see much of her, because she'd left the farm to her younger son while the elder one, my father, who'd quit school at thirteen because he was needed at harvest and seeding, inherited nothing. He never got over that, Grandma leaving him out as if she hadn't held him to her breast, told him stories and, like every mother, waited for his first step, his first word, his bright seeing of the world. No one could come up with a reason why she'd done such a thing. In later years, my mother and I wondered whether my dad would have kept away from the booze if he'd been able to stay on the land. Farming suited him. He loved the solitude and the grandeur of nothing but the sky ahead and all around him as he drove a tractor back and forth across a field, no one but the weather to boss him around, no one but the sun to tell him when to start or stop. Like most farmers, he was a master of tools and engine parts. His other skill was more rare. Neighbours called on him when a horse or a dog needed to be put down and they couldn't bring themselves to pull the trigger. My father was a good shot. One bullet would do the job fast and clean, and such killing never bothered him. Sometimes he'd be paid with a case of beer, other times with a handshake or something the wife had made, a flapper pie or a sealer of canned chicken, the meat encased in jelly.

After the loss of the farm, nothing turned out right for my father. It was the end of the thirties, and he and my mother lived in a cook car abandoned by the CPR on the outskirts of Success. It was better than the homestead shack they'd squatted in just after their wedding. They whitewashed the walls of the cook car and moved in a metal bed and an old folding table with two mismatched chairs. Dad put a shelf in the middle of an apple crate turned sideways and nailed four legs to the bottom. It was Mom's first dresser. Across the front, she tacked a yellow satiny curtain that pulled back and forth on a string.

Dad helped with the combining and pounded fence posts for Shorty Turnbull, his brother-in-law, who owned a farm too big to manage on his own. After the crops were off the fields, Dad shovelled grain for a dollar a day at the

Pool elevator, his saliva black with dust. The jobs were never enough to pull him and Mom out of poverty. When she was pregnant with my brother, she'd knock on the back door of the nearby Chinese café. Cookie, whom Dad had befriended, would give her a bowl of chop suey and a piece of banana cream pie if there was any left over from the day. That's why my brother grew so big and strong, she liked to say. When my parents moved from the train car to Swift Current, thirty miles away, Cookie gave my father a cleaver with an old wooden handle he'd brought with him from China. It was one of the few heirlooms in our family.

After my brother's birth, Dad sold their only cow to pay the hospital bill. One Christmas, he went alone into the country at thirty below with a rifle and shot a coyote, whose hide he sold for five bucks at Western Hide and Fur. He'd set out on foot and was gone so long Mom was afraid he wouldn't come back. The kill bought not only two Dinky Toys for my brother, a tin jack-in-the-box for me and a can of lily of the valley talcum powder that made Mom smell sweet for months, but a bag of oranges that came all the way from somewhere else. On his right hand, frost had bitten his fingers, and they ached in the cold from that day on.

By the time I was in elementary school, Grandma Crozier had become a Mormon. All I knew about her new religion was that she couldn't drink coffee or tea but instead sipped hot water poured from the kettle she kept on the back of the wood stove. Sometimes she'd look straight at me and issue a strange warning: if I ate too many Fudgsicles, I'd lose my hair. Since I wasn't particularly fond of them, I puzzled over the meaning of her words.

Maybe once I'd brought one into her house and let it drip on her floor. Maybe she'd seen me suck the melting chocolate with too much pleasure.

We never went into her tiny bedroom in the back. During our visits, we perched on the edge of the camp bed in the room that served as both living room and kitchen, or we stood near the stove and fridge. A big man with his arms spread could have touched both walls. He'd have had to stoop so his head wouldn't brush the ceiling. I could never remember what we talked about. Grandma probably asked, "How's school," as every adult did, but I wouldn't have told her anything. In the only chair, her swollen leg propped on a stool, she swallowed water with no colour and no flavour, warming something cold inside.

At first I worried her affliction might be genetic, and one day I'd wake up with a leg I had to heft from bed and drag behind me, waves of milk slapping the inner walls of my skin, walleyed, lice-ridden barn cats yowling behind me. Finally I decided it was God's punishment. With perfect irony, he'd smitten her with an excess of sweet maternal liquid—in the breast, a source of nurturance and love; in her leg, a heavy, sour weight that caused suffering, a visible sign of her betrayal of her son and the hurt he would carry into death. I could think of no better vengeance for my father, who loved her anyway and wouldn't have asked for such a thing. *Milk leg,* I whispered inside her little house while the grown-ups talked, *milk leg,* God's righteous anger curdling on my tongue.

first cause: mom and dad

HIS FAVOURITE breakfast is Cream of Wheat. His favourite supper is roast chicken with mashed potatoes. His favourite bread is store-bought white, though your mom bakes her own. His favourite shirt has snap buttons and two pockets, one for cigarettes, one for pens. His favourite pen shows two minks, one on top of the other. It's in the bottom drawer of his side of the dresser, below the hankies your mother washes and irons. You're not supposed to know it's there. His favourite story is how he picked up a semi trailer from the factory in Windsor years ago, drove it through Detroit and all the way to Swift Current without stopping for a sleep. His favourite competition is arm wrestling. He wins all the matches at the Healy Hotel. You wish your arms were as hairy and powerful as his. His favourite expression is "real good." His favourite drink is Pilsner Old Style. Before you could read, you sat on his lap and counted the crows on the label. His favourite TV program is *Don Messer's Jubilee.* He always says, "Look at old Charlie dance." He doesn't have a favourite book. The only thing he reads is the *Swift Current Sun.* He follows the lines with one finger, the nail bitten to the quick, and reads everything three times. You don't know how much he understands.

HER FAVOURITE drink is water from a tap. Her favourite outfit is a loose tank top that covers her belly and a matching pair of shorts with an elastic waist. Her favourite game is curling. She'd miss a wedding or a funeral to watch the final in the Tournament of Hearts. Her favourite dance is the foxtrot. Her favourite dog is still a bull terrier named Patsy that Dad bought when they got married. There are two photographs of her holding your brother at eight months old above Patsy's back as if he were sitting on the dog, but he isn't. Her favourite possession is two Dionne Quintuplet spoons. The letters E-M-I-L-I-E climb from the bowl up the handle on one spoon, C-E-C-I-L-E on the other. Her favourite footwear is the first pair of bowling shoes she could afford to buy, "Goodyear" stamped on the rubber heels. Her favourite place to sit in church is in the balcony, near the back so she can get out fast. She uses her favourite expression to stop you from complaining when you don't get what you want: "It's better than a poke in the eye with a sharp stick." Her favourite place is Saskatchewan: she can't understand why anyone would want to go anywhere else, even for a holiday, even in winter. Her favourite meal is what anyone else in the family wants.

spoilt

AS WELL as practising piano, my friend Ona had to help her mother do the housework every Saturday morning. Their house had two sets of stairs, and it was Ona's job to wash them on her hands and knees with Spic and Span and a stiff brush. Then she had to clean the bathroom and their big verandah with its dozens of windowsills. For this, every Wednesday she got a dime to spend on penny candy at the corner store. I'd beg her for one of her jaw-breakers. Sometimes, dazed with pleasure, I'd forget and bite into the bitter seed at their core. The first time I tasted cardamom, a rush of warmth swept me back to that bliss, my blackened tongue and the click of the sweet shrinking ball against my teeth.

Ona's mom was strict, and their house was spotless. Even their backyard was spotless; it looked as if someone had taken a scrub brush to the sidewalk, the lawn and the daisies and sweet peas Ona's mom had planted instead of potatoes. Ona's stepdad was a pig farmer, though, and every night he parked his truck, the sides splattered with manure and straw, in the driveway at the back. In the truck box rested a huge barrel that he used to haul buttermilk for the pigs. Instead of the scent of sweet peas, it was the rancid smell of sour milk and swine that wafted into the neighbours' yards. And as soon as Ona's stepdad left his truck and walked towards the house, hundreds of flies rose from the ground to drape the buttermilk barrel with a thick, black cloth that buzzed and shifted. It was alien and creepy, and I always cut a wide swath around it.

My mother had a thing about flies. She'd drop what she was doing if she heard a buzzing in the kitchen and go after it. On the farm, before her mother cooked the meat from a slaughtered pig or steer hung in the cold cellar, she'd send one of the kids down to pick off the maggots. That's why Mom's roast beef was cooked to death, all the juices gone into the gravy.

Compared to Ona, I was a spoilt kid. Mom said she didn't know much about mothering; she just wanted me to have a childhood different from her own. My job was to have fun, she said. All she asked me to do was the dusting once a week. To make sure I lifted every ornament and didn't skip any piece of furniture, I'd pretend that the Queen was coming to visit in the afternoon, and I'd picture her running her white-gloved finger over the dresser, the coffee table and the chiffonier. "Good job," she would say in her snooty voice. Then she'd give me a whole quarter to spend on candy. She'd put it heads-up in my palm, her face in profile cameoed into the silvery shine.

Imagining the Queen coming to our house wasn't such a stretch. A few years after the war, she'd passed through Swift Current on the train. My brother had gone to the station with the rest of his Cub pack, and he'd seen her and Prince Philip wave from the platform of the royal car. Whenever I heard the story, I tried to imagine what a royal car would look like. Surely there'd be red velvet everywhere, even on the ceiling. Though it was rude to think of the Queen having to go to the bathroom, the toilet must have been made from solid gold.

There was more to the story than that, though. When the train with its regal passengers pulled out of the station, my brother refused a ride home with the other parents because my father was coming to pick him up. It was a winter night. Barry stood alone on the empty platform, his Cub uniform too thin to stop the cold, the doors of the building locked up, snow swirling along the tracks as if it were a ghost train pulling winter through every town along the line. Dad showed up an hour late, delayed by another round of beer at the Legion. He took my brother to the Venice Café for an orange pop and a big sugar doughnut. My brother pushed the plate away, he said, and Dad got angry. It wasn't every day we got a treat like that. As he got older, that was one of two stories Barry told about our father. The other was about Dad hitting him with the piece of rubber hose that hung like a hollow black snake in the doorway to the cellar. That happened when he was around fifteen. I, not my brother, was the one who cried.

Our father had never wanted children. Mom told us this again and again, as if it were an excuse for his selfishness and neglect. If anyone was to blame, she said, it was her, because she had insisted on it. Dad wasn't a violent man, and he wasn't cruel, but he seemed to feel a love of children would make him unmanly. Once, shortly after my brother was born, Mom and Dad were driving to her parents' farm when she had to pee. She asked Dad to pull over on the side of the road, and then to take the baby. As she was walking back to the car from behind the stubby screen of wolf willow, Dad thrust my brother into her arms. A car was coming down the road; you could see the plume of dust half a mile away, and he didn't want to be seen holding a baby.

It was Mom who spoilt us. Any extra money my father had he spent on himself. "It's too bad he isn't rich," my mother said. "He'd have made a good playboy." He was never too broke to buy a case of beer or to up the ante in a poker game at Shorty Turnbull's farm. Sometimes that meant Mom couldn't buy the things my brother and I thought we needed. Skates, for instance. Second-hand and ill-fitting, mine pinched my toes and made my feet cold. My brother's skates, also hand-me-downs, fit better because he got replacements every year. I didn't feel envious about that, because no matter how hard I tried I was never going to be a good skater. My ankles wobbled. And instead of stopping by flashing my blades to the side as Barry did, I had to fall down before I hit the boards.

My brother excelled at any physical activity, but his best sport was hockey. From the time he was a little kid, people called him a natural. When he joined his first real team, he went to practise in his jeans with nothing to protect his lower legs. The other players, boys from around our neighbourhood, had hockey pants and shin pads. He asked Mom to buy a set of pads for him, but she said we couldn't afford it. She flushed and fidgeted when the coach of the team knocked on our door and spoke to her in the kitchen about her son's talents and the likelihood of injuries if he wasn't properly equipped. My brother never knew how she got the money out of our father or what it cost her, but before his next game at the rink he strapped shin pads over his jeans.

My father would fix a leaking tap, or chop firewood, or repair what was broken, but like most men of his time, he never helped with cooking or any household tasks. When my mom's whole family, all fifteen of them, came in from their farms for Christmas dinner—an event she hosted until her mother died—it was she alone who got up early to stuff the turkey, peel potatoes and turnips and make the pumpkin pies. To get us out from under her feet after we'd opened our presents, she sent Barry and me to the outdoor rink a block away. We'd trudge up the alley, our skates drooped by the laces over one shoulder, snow falling through the early morning darkness, as if we were still in bed and had sunk inside our feather pillows. At the rink, we'd sit on an outdoor bench to pull on our skates. Barry would help me tie mine tight. It was too early for the skating shack, with its pot-bellied stove and its wide-planked floor cut by blades, to be open.

Sometimes my brother would have to clear a path with the big iron snow shovel stuck in a drift by the boards. Then we'd glide onto the bare ice, the only ones there, everything else still and sleepy, one or two houses in the neighbourhood lit. Stars shone bright and cold above us, as if bits of ice had shot from our blades and pierced the blackness. In the soft snow-quiet of early morning, we'd race, he backwards and me forwards. My brother would always win. But I loved the speed when he'd grab my arm, twirl me around like a spinning top and then let me go.

After our Christmas dinner, which we ate around four o'clock, Mom and my aunts cleaned up. My brother, cousins and I and all the men were free to do what we wanted. We kids played with our new toys in the hallway or in my parents' bedroom. Mom had set up the kitchen table in the living room for the turkey dinner. Now that it was done, the men hunched around two card tables, where the youngest kids had sat to eat half an hour before, and played whist. The women joined in only when the last plates sat clean in the cupboard and they had made turkey sandwiches with Mom's homemade buns for a late-night lunch. One aunt sliced dill pickles, and Mom spooned cranberries into the mustard dish her older brother had sent from England before he died in the war. His ship had collided with an Allied boat in the cold Atlantic night, and he and all of his crew went down.

Like Ona's mother, Mom set Saturday morning aside to clean the house. And every Monday—no matter what happened in the family, the town or the world outside—was washday. Monday mornings my mother woke up and took note of the weather, though not even a heavy rain or the temperature falling to thirty below could stop the washing from getting done. As she pulled on her housecoat, she hoped it would be sunny and there'd be a wind. But not too much of one, because then the clothes could be yanked from the line.

For hours in the cellar, she'd run one load after another through the wringer of the washer with its two laundry tubs, then trudge up the narrow wooden stairs with a basket of wet laundry and out the back door to the clothesline. Some days it was so cold she had to wear a parka with a hood. She never asked me to help, and like a princess from a storybook, I felt put out when I had to walk across the cellar to get a jar of preserves from the shelf, the floor slippery with soapy water from the draining tub. On washdays, though, I knew better than to complain about anything, even an upset stomach or a cold coming on. My mother had a don't-you-dare-bother-me look about her, and if she spoke at all, her voice was taut and barbed, like a wire fence meant to keep you out.

After taking Dad's frozen shirts from the line, my mother would prop them on the couch to dry. At first, stiff from the cold, they held the shape of a body, the torso of a soldier with his legs blown off. When the bloodless arms, chests and shoulders began to thaw, the shirts collapsed, the breath gone out of them. No matter what the temperature, when my brother and his friends came home from school for lunch, they'd play war in the yard in trenches they'd dug out of snow. They built guns out of kindling and lobbed spruce cones that exploded when they hit the ground. Banished from the game because I was a girl and so much younger, I'd watch them from the window.

After a while, bored with the battles in the yard, I'd cut ladies from last year's summer catalogue, trying to find a whole one I could use as a paper doll. These ladies didn't wear housedresses, like my mother and the other women on our block, but fancy suits or dressing gowns. When you could see their feet, they were elegant in high heels or slippers with puffs of pink fur over the toes. In the snow, my brother and his friends staggered, died, then got up again. To the side of the house, my mother hung the next load on the line, sheet after sheet and then the towels, her hands red, one clothespin, then another, clenched between her teeth.

familiar
as salt

OUT OF our big front window I could see the ghost of the moon, sunlight still smouldering low in the sky. I balanced a red potato in the palm of my hand. It was just before supper, and the smell of roasting chicken wafting from the kitchen made me ravenous. When I held the potato between my fingers and up to the window, it eclipsed the moon's milky light. I could hear the snicks of a knife and thud after thud as Mom sliced the seed potatoes and dropped them into a bucket by the kitchen sink. She made sure each piece had an eye.

At the table we filled our plates with mashed potatoes and creamed corn from a can. Dad always took my special piece of chicken, the smallest piece of white meat with the wishing bone inside, but I'd sneak it from his plate and he'd pretend he didn't see. He carved the breast meat for himself and gave Barry both the legs. Mom claimed a thigh and the Pope's nose, the polyp of fat and crispy skin that stuck out from the back end where the tail used to be. The four of us soaked everything with gravy Mom made from the drippings. The gravy was the best part of any meat Mom roasted.

After supper, my brother left the house for a marble tournament in the schoolyard; Dad sipped a beer. I cleaned the table and helped Mom with the dishes. Then we headed out to the yard. It had always been my brother who helped with the planting. But now I was old enough. In the porch I pulled on my rubber boots; Dad, his leather workboots with the hard toes; Mom, an old pair of curling shoes with the laces gone. Dad had tilled our long back garden the week before. The ground was dark and damp. Every spring when the snow melted, runoff streamed down the alley and pooled in that end of the yard. The tops of my boots rolled down so I'd look like a pirate, I waded into it until water leaked inside and soaked my socks.

Mom had planted the seeds for peas and beans on her own a few days before. Our task now was the potatoes. We started at the far end near the alley. Dad dug a hole, Mom dropped a piece of potato in, Dad let the dirt slide from his shovel to cover it, and I stamped the mound of earth flat. I followed my parents row after row, looking back after each was done to see my footprints mapping the spots where the green would push through. One potato, two potatoes, three potatoes, four. We worked through the twilight, our feet sinking in the turned earth. No one talked. My parents didn't get mad at each other. We each had our job to do. Five potatoes, six potatoes, seven potatoes, more. The planting couldn't have been done without me.

AFTER THE FIRST growth appeared, each stem and leaf erupting through the soil with the force of a small volcano, I walked down the rows beside Mom. She watered the plants with a black rubber hose. As the plants filled out, we'd peer closely at the leaves, checking for potato bugs.

They had tan heads and orange-yellow backs with vertical black stripes, as if they'd dressed in their best dinner jackets for their juicy meal. Mom dropped the bugs we found into a large corn-syrup can with a few inches of kerosene in the bottom. I loved to crack them between my fingers first. We'd check the underside of leaves for tiny orange eggs that I'd squash. The ones we missed would hatch into larvae, horrid creatures that looked like a cross between a slug and a ladybug, two rows of black dots along each side, their red backs soft and sticky.

In late summer, after Mom had picked the peas and beans, she announced it was time to dig up the potatoes. She'd stopped watering by then, and the ground was dry. Dad dug near the bushy plants and pulled the tops. He and Mom collected the big potatoes underneath and dropped them into a bucket. I stayed behind while they moved to the next plant, reached my hands into the dark earth and scrounged for the small potatoes they didn't get. Some the size of jaw breakers, others of robins' eggs, they were beautiful, and I knew they were the best to eat, boiled in their skins and drizzled with butter. But I didn't find harvesting potatoes as much fun as stomping them into the earth or killing the bugs that devoured their leaves. After a row or two, I ran to the alley to play with my friends.

MOM'S GOAL every year was to grow enough potatoes to last us through the winter. That wasn't easy, because every day was potato day at our house. I hated peas from a can, I'd refuse a cooked carrot, but I never turned down a potato, boiled or mashed or scalloped, sliced and fried in bacon fat or pulped with a fork for the topping of shepherd's pie. Mom would mix new potatoes with fresh peas and cook them in a cream sauce made from butter, flour, milk, and lots of salt and pepper. My father always asked for that. When he got throat cancer in his early fifties, and the cobalt dried up his saliva, few of his other favourite foods would be moist enough to swallow.

We couldn't eat all the potatoes we grew, though. We had to save enough for planting. The seed potatoes were the ones at the bottom of the bin in the cellar. As the months passed, their fresh, outdoor odour gave way to fetid. The potatoes softened and turned wet and brown, as if we'd dug them from the muck of a slough instead of the parched summer soil. From the potato bin, they'd send out pale sprouts like underwater feelers, looking for the light that couldn't reach them.

I never questioned why we ate so many potatoes. But the potatoes served for supper at my friend's houses were definitely a different kind. Our garden's earthy signature—the coldness of the ground in spring, the runoff from the alley, water from our hose, and the dirt my father sweetened with manure from my grandparents' farm—was as familiar as the salt I licked from the sun-browned skin on my forearms. They were our potatoes, and I had helped make them. I had seen their beginning in the moon's frail light.

my soul
to keep

OUR NEIGHBOURHOOD had no fences. Front yards spilled one into the other, and I could cut across them from my house to the end of the street, sometimes following a path worn by the feet of the older kids through a caragana hedge that tried to create a border. Not much went on in front of the houses. The artery of the block was the alley where we gathered after school and on weekends to play kick the can or run-sheep-run or anti-ay-over, bouncing the ball over the roof of my parents' collapsing garage. Because the front was more private, Ona and I chose a spot at the edge of her verandah under one of her mother's roses as a graveyard. The ground was soft there, and the roses, with their short lives and their stems whose bite drew blood from our fingers, seemed to be the perfect graveyard flower.

The summer Ona was seven and I was eight, we scouted the sidewalks and gutters for the dead: a bird fallen from a nest or gutted by a cat, a moth with torn wings, or, when we were desperate, an ant or a dried-up earthworm who'd been stopped mid-crawl after the rain. Both of us went to Sunday school, she at the Lutheran Church at the top of

Central Avenue and me at First United, about six blocks away. We were learning about resurrection. We were learning about bodies rising from the earth at the sound of a trumpet and climbing the clouds to heaven. Both of us knew there'd be cotton candy there and fat little angels that looked exactly like our pink plastic dolls, except that the celestial beings had wings and eyelids that wouldn't click when they opened and closed.

For crosses we stuck together two Popsicle sticks with Elmer's Glue or, for a small creature like an ant, two toothpicks. Sometimes we'd cover the wood with foil Dad gave me from his pack of cigarettes. A lucky find was a single earring Ona's mother didn't want anymore, a flattened pearl disk the size of a nickel. We saved it to use as a tombstone for a bird.

Because we didn't have boxes small enough to coffin our dead, we collected the fluff from the cottonwood tree that bordered our two yards near the front wooden walk. We'd pinch together a soft nest to put the body in, then cover it with more downy seeds. From our cutlery drawer, I'd stolen a tablespoon to dig with; my mom was the least likely of our parents to notice or to get mad if she did. With every burial we said a prayer, the scary one I recited every night before I fell asleep. Ona didn't know it, but she was quick to learn.

> *Now I lay me down to sleep*
> *I pray the Lord my soul to keep*
> *If I should die before I wake*
> *I pray the Lord my soul to take.*

We'd fill the cap of a pill bottle with water and another one with the tiny green peas from inside a caragana pod, set these beside the graves, then wait. The creatures we'd buried would want to eat and drink when they woke up. Because I got out of bed earlier than Ona, I was the first there in the morning. Day after day, though, nothing happened. The silver crosses glinted in the early sunlight, the ground was undisturbed. We heard no trumpet, just my brother practising his trombone in our living room. The sounds that drifted through the open window wouldn't have caused anyone to be born again.

One morning we decided to dig up the grave of a robin we'd found smashed below Ona's front window. At first we thought it was alive; its chest was moving. Just before I picked it up, Ona shrieked, "It's worms!" The breast writhed with small red whips. We quickly stuck the robin back in the ground and banged our hands down hard on the dirt. Though we didn't talk about it, that was the end of our graveyard. We weren't as crestfallen as we could have been, because as of yet, there was no personal connection. No pet of ours had died. The desiccated, broken, stepped-on or torn-apart were strangers. The animal closest to us, my family's dog, Tiny, had been with us at most burials. She lay beside us on the grass, alert and watchful as the mythical dog I didn't know about then who guards the gate to the underworld.

Our role as undertakers led Ona and me into our first and last business venture. In stealing the caps of pill bottles to use as miniature bowls for the victuals of the dead, we'd noticed that the wad of cotton on the top looked exactly like the cottonwood fluff we'd used to pillow the bodies. The fluff also resembled the narrow sheet of cotton batten scrolled in long blue paper that sat in our medicine cabinet. Mom would tear off a piece to hold over my ear when my eardrum broke after hours of pain, the pus running out of it. Earaches were one of my torments.

Ona and I dragged a wooden chair from her kitchen and picked cotton from the big tree's lowest branches. I'd dumped the inch or two of cocoa from the tin I'd found in Mom's pantry and washed it out. We picked until the tin was full.

At the end of our block and across a busy street stood Ralph's Food Market. Everyone in the vicinity shopped for groceries there, and the cashier, Mrs. Murphy, knew all the local kids. Ralph, the owner, let customers charge what they bought. Mom settled her bill every month so she wouldn't get behind, but many of our neighbours, those better off than us, never paid, and Ralph often had trouble making the rent.

Tiny always came with me when Mom sent me for a loaf of bread or a can of peas. She'd sit on the corner on the slight rise of the McMurchies' lawn at the end of our block. In the firm voice I'd learned from my brother, I'd tell her to stay. We didn't want her running into traffic. From the store window I could see her as faithful and still as the statue of Greyfriars Bobby I'd seen in a book. The store workers smiled when they looked at her, and they'd say something nice to me. Tiny stared intently as I crossed the street to her, then ran ahead of me, doubling back to urge me on as we made our way home.

With Tiny at her usual place on the corner, Ona and I waited politely in the grocery line until we were at the register. We showed Mrs. Murphy our cocoa can of cotton and said we wanted to sell it. She pried off the lid and looked inside. "This is worth a dime," she said. That was enough for both of us to buy a Popsicle.

"That's great," I said. "We'll be back with more!"

"I think that's all we're going to need right now. I'll let you know when we run short."

I knew by the look on her face—a mix of amusement and kindness—that waiting for a request for more cotton would be like waiting for the birds and worms and insects to rise from the ground and wing their way to heaven.

TINY DIED seven years later, shortly after we'd moved across town to a different, shabbier house and I'd started high school. Ralph's Food Market had closed by then, and the Pioneer Co-op had taken over.

No one prayed, and no one buried her. My brother, the one she loved most, had left home by then. Dad, who'd sold his rifle and didn't put down animals any more, took her to the vet when she couldn't stand up one morning. She was thirteen. Mom and I cried as Dad wrapped Tiny in a towel so she wouldn't bite and carried her to the car, her red pointed ears poking above the terrycloth. He didn't bring her back. I didn't ask where she'd ended up. I didn't want to know.

crazy
city kid

LONG AFTER my brother wanted to stay home on Sundays with his friends, I still loved our country outings. When Mom and I got home from church—Dad never went—we'd change out of our good clothes, then make the thirty-mile drive to her parents' farm near Success, Dad at the wheel. I never heard my father gripe about these visits. Maybe he felt grateful that his in-laws welcomed him. Since his mother had signed over the Crozier farm to his brother, Dad hadn't set foot on the land his father had homesteaded, just a few miles down and across the road from where Mom had grown up.

For hours, my cousins Diane and Lou-Anne and I would sweep and decorate and make tea in an abandoned wooden granary we'd turned into a playhouse. There were no windows, but we'd nailed a thrown-out curtain on the wall to make a pretend one, and we kept the small door open. We had our own fly swatter, its rubber flap cracked and limp, and a curled, sticky ribbon hung from the ceiling. You couldn't tell what colour the ribbon had been originally. Now it was black with old dead flies.

Uncle Lyn stored a rusted pot-bellied stove inside the granary. With its detached tin chimney pipe it took up most of the room, but it was perfect for the imaginary meals we cooked for the imaginary crew that came at harvest time. We saved Black Magic boxes from Christmas and patted mud into the pleated paper cups to make chocolates. Several times we coaxed Diane and Lou-Anne's youngest brother to eat one, and he didn't even make a face. There was always a barn cat begging to be fed, a different one each summer, sometimes with the tip of an ear torn off by another cat, its fur ragged. We'd tame the cat enough to come inside and lick cream from an old saucer with the pattern worn off, but it would never let us pet it.

My favourite part of the day was the killing of the chicken for Sunday supper. Nothing that bloody or exciting took place at our house in town. Grandma would pick out the bird she wanted from the hen coop, and Grandpa would grab it around the wings, flop it onto the chopping block and cut off its head with a hatchet, leaving the neck intact. The cousins and I leaped back to avoid the spurting blood while the chicken flapped madly around the yard, almost flying. Grandma told us the bird was trying to carry its own soul up to its maker. She often said funny things like that. She'd been born in what they called the Old World, in her case Wales, and she'd passed on a lot of superstitions to her children. On New Year's Day, for instance, a woman couldn't be the first person to walk through the door or your household would be cursed. A shoe left on a table at any time of the year brought bad luck to the owner of the house. Though Grandma never mentioned the effects of getting splattered red by a headless chicken, I thought that would surely be the worst, a hex that could last a lifetime. That didn't worry my boy cousins, who ran after the chicken till it skidded to a stop in the dust and fell down dead.

By then, my two other aunts and their husbands had arrived at the farm. Once they'd greeted one another and talked about the weather, all the men, including my dad, left the house to "check the crops." Uncle Lyn always said this with a big grin. He was the youngest of Mom's siblings, and he acted goofy and boyish when Grandpa was around. Uncle Lyn was the only one who paid attention to me and my cousins in our playhouse. Sometimes he'd stop by for tea, pouring golden whiskey into his cup from a mickey tucked in his overalls and sticking out his little finger as he gripped the handle to make us laugh.

Once the men had gone outside, the women got to work in the kitchen. Auntie Glad, the oldest of Mom's sisters, told Grandma to sit at the table. "Get off your feet for a while," she said in her bossy voice. "We can do this without you." I sat beside Grandma because Auntie Glad, who didn't have kids herself, hated it when her nieces or nephews got in the way. My Aunt Kitty, who, according to Mom, had got the best of everything when they were kids, scalded the chicken in a big pot of hot water on the wood stove to loosen the feathers. The sisters took turns plucking, then pulled out the pinfeathers. Mom passed the naked bird over the flames that sparked and hissed from the stove's open burner to singe the hairs. The smell in the kitchen reminded me of the time my brother had burned the hairs on his arm with a cigarette lighter, only worse. It was hard to imagine that the roasting chicken would soon smell so good.

The best part of all came next. My mom and my aunts, for no reason I could understand, gave me first dibs to clean out the inside of the chicken. My cousins thought I was the crazy city kid, but I didn't care. I loved reaching my hand inside the warm hen and pulling out the slippery package of intestines, gizzard, heart, liver and sometimes, if I was lucky, a string of small, translucent eggs, pale yellow and firm between the fingers but without the hard shell.

After supper, before we left for home, I'd sometimes go with Grandma to lock the chickens in for the night. I let her herd them on her own from the run into the coop, swinging her apron in front of her. I didn't get too close; there was one hen who'd tried many times to peck the freckles on my ankles. Grandma raked out the old straw, and I helped her scatter the new. She let me toss yellow seeds from a burlap sack onto the dirt floor. I jumped back as the hens rushed towards the feed. Outside the coop, Grandma closed and snibbed the door. "Sleep tight, girls," she said.

Grandma walked back to the house after that, but I stayed behind until the hens had finished eating, staring through the screen that covered half the door to let in the fresh night air. Some of the hens seemed to hover in the dusk of the coop. I knew they were perched, but I couldn't make out the rafters. Their feathers seemed brighter than during the day, as if a flashlight had caught one after another in its electric eye. The smell was almost indescribable: a whiff of wet feathers, though they were dry now; dust that had tufted from their feet when they'd pecked the seeds; an acrid pungency from the white droppings that spotted the floor. Every few seconds there'd be a soft cluck, then silence, and a sound close to whispering. What was the secret they were sharing?

It would be a few years before I sat in squirmy silence with the other grade 8 girls to watch a film about "human reproduction." We learned there were eggs inside our bodies too, so small most of us would never get to see them. Were they as beautiful, I wondered, when magnified and held up to the light? Watching the dust motes flicker in the projector's beam, I dreamed myself back to my grandmother's kitchen, my hand warm with blood as I pulled from the hen the necklace of tiny eggs, singular and lovely as amber beads. How I longed for something as exquisite inside me.

first cause: rain

THERE'S RARELY ENOUGH of it, though in a deluge
it floods basements and roads and barns and crops and
a city underpass where once a woman, trapped in her
car, drowned on a day that began with blue skies and no
weather warning. It can be a malevolent mercy, keeping
a farmer off the field for half a season; a hard baptism,
dropping crystal pebbles on your skin, flattening the
ripened crops, the most bountiful in twenty years. It can
be lifted up by wind, come at you horizontal or fall halfway, then evaporate and never hit the ground. The name
for that is *virga*.

Rain takes any mood you want to give it: sadness
or grief or exaltation or the longing for a lover far from
home. For all its noise, it has never had its own language.
It sounds only when it strikes, a mynah bird calling its
notes from tin Quonsets, wooden shingles on a shed, wolf-
willow leaves, the hoods of slickers, car roofs, the glass of
skyscrapers, the canvas of a tent, water running or standing still. For centuries on the plains, it has made the people
dance. It has made them stamp the ground like bison, lift
their faces to the sky and build the fires they call rain
down to douse.

first cause: snow

SNOW FALLS slowly in memory. It is tentativeness given form and temperature, seeming again and again to hesitate, not knowing what lies below, whether the surface will be slippery or smooth, level or steep, a hillside, a field of purple clover, an open mouth. The snowflakes fall and lift, then fall again, the first ones melting as they touch the ground. Those that follow retain their shapes, remain as they were when they feathered the sky. One by one they accumulate, form a density of stars, a thousand nameless constellations, none of them bruising or breaking, not a word, not a sigh. Their whole purpose is to fall, to settle down. A parking lot, a birch grove, a woman's hair. No thought can stop the snow, no panegyric or lament. Even if you're sleeping, you know the sky is white with down. To the world outside your window, it brings a riddled hush, a new religion, everything has been touched but touched softly, without hands.

first cause: sky

ABOVE YOU, the sky is a vast blue wonder, something
held tight in the chest and then released to rush like
the breath of a god, quickening the grasslands into stark,
bewildering beauty. The sky is skinless yet animate,
strangely expectant. It is waiting for something to happen.
Some days anvil-shaped clouds ride the horizon—lightning
leaps from field to field, spears through a window, splits
a tree, blows off the hooves of cattle near the dugout.
You see it long before you hear a sound. When at last the
thunder booms, it drums the ground and the mirrors
in the houses tremble.

Calm or restless, the sky follows your every step.
It touches you with loneliness. It humbles your tongue.
Nothing is taller, more open. It makes you fall in love with
weather, with nimbus and feather and hollow bone. Under
its blue gaze, you mark the smallest thing: a lichen scab
on stone, thin legs of a crab spider on the petal of a rose,
a snowdrift on the beak of a chickadee. Though you lower
your head, your prayers go upwards. Imagine all the
praise and fear and doubt the sky must hold.

a spell of
lilacs

O N EITHER side of the six steps that led to our front door, two lilac bushes exploded into fragrant blossom every spring. The bushes were so wide and tall we called them trees. In late May the branches bowed low, and the blossoms brushed across your hair when you walked beneath them. If you were the romantic kind, like some of my brother's girlfriends, their scent could make you swoon. Even strangers passing by stopped to admire the lilacs. Sometimes they knocked on our door to ask if they could pick them. Mom always went out with a knife Dad kept sharpened for that purpose and cut a huge bouquet.

The opposite of frugality, the lilacs made us special; they hid the poverty of the house, the messy yard, the worry that lived inside the walls. My mother could give and give; her natural generosity had a chance to show itself. I couldn't walk by the bushes without burying my face in the purple flowers and inhaling deeply, taking in with the scent my mother's pleasure, her small pride in being able to bestow on whoever asked such a lush and momentary beauty.

In many family photographs, my brother and I stand in front of the lilacs. There's one of him at around thirteen with his first new baseball glove, me small beside him, my skinny legs bare. There's another of him posing in the spiffy pants and shirt he wore to his grade 8 graduation, and one of me seven years later for the same occasion in a blue dress my grandmother Ford had sewn. I hated that dress. Though my grandmother was an expert seamstress, the sleeves didn't lie flat at the shoulders, and she'd bought enough material to sew exactly the same dress for my two younger cousins, who were only in grades 6 and 7. My mother always said Grandma liked them better than she liked me, and this seemed the proof.

Twice, I posed as a flower girl in front of the lilacs. The first time, at five, I wore a diaphanous yellow, the colour of a cabbage butterfly. After Mom snapped the picture, I ran to the backyard and pumped myself high on the swing, feeling light and lovely in the skirt that puffed out from my legs, then flattened, puffed out and flattened again. From the porch next door, Ona called me over. I skipped towards her, thinking she wanted a better look at how pretty I was. When I got close, she stepped outside and hit me on the head with a piece of firewood. "You think you're so great," she said, and banged the door shut.

I ran home crying, not sure what had happened, my hand on my head, my fingers sticky with blood from the scrape. In the kitchen, my mother got me out of the yellow dress then pulled the kitchen table over to the sink. She lifted me up and laid me on my back so she could wash my hair, careful with the sore spot. "You'll feel pretty again," she said. "Wait till you get to wear your headband of flowers." They weren't real flowers like the lilacs, but made of some kind of satiny material, flat and overlapping as if they'd been pressed inside a book. As soon I donned the headband, my head stopped hurting. Besides, I knew I'd gone far enough with self-pity. My mother's "If you don't stop crying, I'll give you something to cry about" was something I heard too often to keep snivelling for long.

The bride, Doris, who'd chosen me for her flower girl, was one of the three Andrews sisters who rented the upstairs rooms in our house, with their mother. They came in from their farm in late fall and stayed through the winter. Their brother remained in the old house on the land. He seeded the crops and drove the combine during the harvest, though Dad said the sisters worked like men on the farm, raising pigs and calves, fixing barbed-wire fences and driving the grain truck in the fields to catch the wheat streaming from the hopper. I looked forward to their move to our house every year. More often than not, it was the first snow that announced their arrival. In the spring, their return to the country coincided with the delivery to our front door of a box of downy yellow chicks. Until the Andrews left a few days later, they kept the chicks upstairs under a low light bulb they'd rigged up. I'd dip my hands into the warm, soft pool and scoop one out to hold in my palm. It was like a small ball of sunshine that had sprouted feathers.

With the Brownie box camera Mom had acquired by saving coupons from Nabob tea, she took a picture of

Doris in her white bridal gown in front of the lilacs. Two years later I wore blue taffeta as a flower girl for her sister, Myrtle. The dress came with a blue, three-layered crinoline that I would later wear when I twirled like a ballerina on the linoleum in front of our couch. Different blooms on the same bushes beautified the backdrop in the two pictures, which Mom hung on the wall of her bedroom. Seeing the lilacs behind and above me made my nostrils flare every time I looked at the black-and-white photos in their wooden frames.

The two Andrews sisters were in their forties when they became brides, and no one had expected them to get married. Their older sister, Winnie, never did. I liked her the best, but my favourite of the Andrews was their mother, whom I called Grandma. In the morning, when I'd hear footsteps creak on the ceiling above my cot in the corner of my parents' room, I'd sneak upstairs in my flannelette pyjamas, knock on Grandma's bedroom door and be invited in. I'd climb beside her under the covers, and Winnie would bring both of us a cup of tea. Sometimes as a treat I'd get a piece of toast spread with jam. Grandma showed me how to roll it up, then dunk the end into the tea before taking a bite. It was a most elegant breakfast; I felt ladylike beside her. Grandma spoke with an English accent, and we always had matching saucers for our cups.

Mom worried that I was bugging the Andrews, and she told them to let her know if I was getting underfoot. I learned on my own to judge if I wasn't welcome. There was never a problem with Winnie, who was the least fussy of the sisters and the handiest on the farm. Mom said Winnie could throw a steer for branding without her brother's help. Doris would sometimes pinch her lips when she saw me about to walk into their hallway. Myrtle might go about her business and refuse to meet my eye. When either thing happened, I'd pretend I was there to use the toilet to the left of the stairs; it was the only one in the house.

Some evenings I'd go back upstairs, in my pyjamas again, and sit on Grandma's bed. She'd never turn me out. Every night, in a long white nightgown, she sat in front of her mirror on the stool that slid from the space in between the two pedestals of her dresser. She'd remove the bobby pins, one by one, from the bun coiled at the back of her neck and put them in a little porcelain box with a gold scroll around the rim and a red rose flaring in the centre. I loved the bobby pins. How gentle and thoughtful was the man who invented them: he'd rounded the metal tips with bulbs of plastic so they wouldn't scratch Grandma's head. Her hair spilled over her shoulders like the wisps of snow the wind blew across the roads in winter.

I dangled my feet over the edge of her bed as I watched Grandma brush her hair. The back of the brush was ivory, a white glow with a haze of yellow in it as if it had been polished by my dad's fingers, the ones he used to hold a cigarette. I couldn't believe how dazzling her hair was and didn't understand why she tucked it away every morning. When she put the brush down, I jumped off the bed and watched her climb under the covers. Her hair fanned out on the pillow, her face framed in its silky white. "Sleep tight, little girl," she'd say. That was my signal to reply,

64

"Don't let the bed bugs bite," then slip from her room, close her door and go down to my own small bed. Sometimes I'd slide down the banister, the quietest way to descend, as if I were a burglar and had stolen something precious from the upstairs rooms.

Ona and Lynda didn't understand how it was possible for me to have three grandmothers. I felt lucky, especially as Grandma Andrews was by far the best of them. There were no bad stories about her like the ones I overheard my parents tell about Grandma Ford and Grandma Crozier. She'd never sent any of her children away or disinherited them. And if she had sewn my grade 8 graduation dress, I knew it would have been just for me. She wouldn't have made copies for my cousins.

On her daughters' wedding days, Grandma Andrews posed in front of the lilacs too. In both photos, she wore the same plain dress with buttons up the front, a thin belt, lisle stockings and black, laced-up shoes with a short heel. Her hair disappeared into her usual bun, above which perched a little black hat that looked like a conductor's except for the veil that puffed from the back. I liked to think of her calling, "All aboard," and I'd jump on the train beside her.

Grandma died three years after she and Winnie stopped renting our upstairs rooms. Mom said I was too young to attend her funeral. Pushing myself back and forth on the swing when all the adults were in church, I wondered if Winnie had brushed her mother's hair and spread it on a satin pillow. I wished I could have placed her bobby pins in their small box beside her in the coffin and blessed her with a handful of lilacs. I'd have shaken a bouquet over her head and down the length of her, the way a priest shakes his censer to sprinkle holy water. She'd have carried the insistent fragrance and tiny black seeds with her no matter how far she had to travel. Around her sleeping body, they'd have cast their lilac spell in the darkest tunnels of the earth.

fox and
goose

IT DIDN'T TAKE LONG to get to the western outskirts of town and onto the road that led to my grandparents' farm. We'd pass the two grain elevators, shoulders sloped, beside the railroad tracks; the John Deere dealership with its gleaming green machines that looked like giant mutant insects; the horse plant where Dad had worked one winter (I didn't want to know what daily happened there); the stockyard with its nostril-burning stench, and finally, a long wooden shed fallen in on one side. It looked like a barn for pigs—I'd seen them in other places—but Dad said it had been a fox farm.

A farm for foxes! I imagined dozens of them like Grandpa's cows lying peaceful in a pasture, walking in single file towards the water trough, or stretching and yawning like barn cats as they woke from a nap. I thought they must have been pets like Tiny, who resembled a fox with her pointed nose, perky upright ears and long red coat. No, Dad said, they were raised for their hides. To make coats and hats for fancy ladies.

I didn't like to think of their fur being ripped from their flesh to make something else look sleek and plush and shiny. I was glad the shed that housed the animals had collapsed. Dad said that the owner, when he knew he couldn't save his business, opened the pens and let the remaining foxes go. They'd been bred for beauty: he'd raised not only red but silver foxes and grey and blue and black ones. Farmers who owned land close by, Dad said, still talked of seeing them. Though they worried about their chickens, they were often startled into wonder by a slurry of blue against the bluer sky or a spill of silver rippling through the tall grasses. In the car, I closed my eyes and saw dusk-coloured foxes slip through the twilight, then disappear like smoke into the place of dreams I fell into every night. Even there, where they could settle softly inside my sleep, there was nothing I could do to keep them safe.

ONCE WINTER arrived, the backyard's tall yellow grasses my father never scythed caught the snow and held it. On mornings when the flakes in their falling grew as big as the paper ones we stuck to classroom windows, the neighbourhood kids tumbled from doorways. One behind the other, we tromped a circle in the snow with our boots, turning the yard into a white meadow for geese to run in, flapping their blunt wings, a fox in hot pursuit.

The most important word in the game was *home*. Home was the centre of the circle, and when you landed there, after whipping down one of several spokes, you were safe. The fox couldn't touch you. The problem was you were free from harm for only a moment: another goose fleeing for its life could force you out, back onto the dangerous circumference pocked with our tracks like the face of the moon.

Racing through the cold, parkas undone, faces flushed, my friends and I would have thrown off our scarves by now. They'd be scattered outside the circle like the skins of long improbable snakes, yellow, blue, green, white with wide red stripes. The spots where our mouths had soaked the wool hardened into disks of ice as the sun slid lower in the sky.

As we skittered and slipped and darted to the centre, we lost who we were, lost our names and the names of our mothers who had sent us out to play. We were legs and lungs and big hearts pumping. We were geese; one of us, a fox. No one in the game broke the rules. We never called "Time out!" We never stepped from the circle to catch our breath. How essential was that form we had drawn with our boots, how perfect and invariable, how charged with frenzy and delicious dread.

As geese, we shrieked with panic and joy and ran and ran—for our lives, we thought. But that wasn't it. The fox mustn't catch you not because he'll eat you up but because he wants to change places. He wants to touch you, to lose his fur and teeth, to grow feathers, to flee with the others, the hot musty breath of the new fox beating on the back of his neck. And suddenly—sure-footed on your paws—that is you. Cunning and radiant against the snow, you feel a different blood burning bright inside you as you leap to catch a wing.

tasting
the air

AT RECESS the boys would go crazy. They'd push us off the swings or pelt us with snowballs with stones in the centre. Every winter, at least one boy would stick his tongue on the metal of the monkey bar at another boy's dare, and a girl would run to get a teacher while tears and mucus froze on his face. It was common for the boys, like barbarian marauders, to invade our space near the girls' entrance, grab a girl and pinch her or yank the barrettes from her hair. They'd grip your forearm just above your wrist and twist the skin. It was called a snake-bite, and it hurt a lot. I felt safe around the roughest boys, though, because my brother protected me. His reputation for toughness was so ingrained that even when he'd left for high school on the other side of town, I just had to say, "I'm Barry Crozier's sister," and the bullies would leave me be.

The worst bully went to St. Pat's, the Catholic school across the road. His name was Larry, and he lived down our alley in a big two-storey of red brick, which wasn't really brick but sheets of tar siding with a red gritty surface and grey lines pressed in a grid to look like mortar. In the swimming pool he'd throw himself on top of me, push me under with his arms and chest till I thought I'd drown.

My friend Lynda said it meant he liked me, but it didn't feel that way.

There was something wrong with Larry. Adults noticed it too. He was sneaky, and he assumed he could get away with anything. He had red hair, which my mother said was a sign of temper. She thought his parents let him run wild. They went out a lot, she said, and left their kids to fend for themselves. *Fend* was a word I liked, though I wasn't sure what it might mean.

Larry was tall and gangly, his bones seeming to grow more quickly than the rest of him, his skin stretched pale and thin and freckled. Maybe he wasn't fending well, I thought, and he'd keep growing taller, his skin more transparent, until one day we'd see right through him, as if he wasn't there. I wished for that. Some afternoons as I pumped myself higher and higher on our tall wooden swing, which my dad had salvaged from a city playground when they replaced it with a stunted metal version, Larry would steal up from behind and start to push. He'd clutch the chains to suspend me high in the air and slide one hand over my bare legs. I wiggled and tried to kick him, and finally he'd let me drop to where my feet could touch the ground. I knew what he did was wrong, but I didn't tell anyone. I feared what he'd do to get even.

One Saturday morning I was walking down the alley to Lynda's house, a chalk to draw a hopscotch in my jacket pocket along with a special stone to throw, when Larry came around the corner with one of his buddies from the Catholic school. In front of him, in both hands, Larry held a garter snake, green with a pale belly, a red stripe streaking down each side like threads of blood. It was too late for me to disappear. I raced towards my house, the boys chasing me, Larry's friend yelling, "Drop it down her back!" I knew I'd up and die if the snake slid down my spine. When I stumbled, Larry grabbed me. One hand grasped my jacket by the back of the collar—how sick I felt—and the long slick belly sluiced across my neck. I twisted in his grip and screamed. Above the fear that roared in my head, I heard my brother's voice: "Let her go."

Like a hero in a cowboy movie, he walked from our yard into the alley. He must have been on his way to baseball practice; the glove on his hand made his fist look like Popeye's. The boys stared at him. Larry pulled the snake away. I hadn't noticed before that the boy I didn't know held a hammer. My brother reached for me, turned his back on them and led me down our wooden walk, past the swing and into the back porch. "Mom's home," he said. "Go inside." He went out again past the boys and up the alley towards the baseball diamond. "I'll see you later," he said to Larry, who didn't talk back.

I waited a few minutes, then snuck out low and quiet and hunkered behind the woodpile at the back of our house. The boys had already forgotten about me. Larry handed the snake to his friend, who stretched it out to its full length—two feet or so—against a telephone pole. It glistened in the light like the new skin on my arms and shoulders when they peeled after a sunburn. Larry reached in his pocket, pulled out two nails and, with the hammer, pounded the snake into the wood. It twisted on those two metal spikes, unable to crawl out of its pain. Everything fell silent; even the wind lay down in the grass and held its breath. The boys stood not knowing what to do, their stupid hands dangling from their wrists, the beautiful green mouth opening, a terrible dark O no one could hear. I loved it then, that snake.

After that morning, my fear of snakes left for good. By the creek I would seek them out, watch them sip water among the stones with a delicacy that made me shiver. Their thin red tongues seemed to taste the air, the morning and the evening, the darkness at the heart of things.

spit

SPIT, sb., a small, low tongue of land projecting onto water; a shuttle pin; a straight horizontal stroke used as a marking in books; the fluid secreted by the glands of the mouth.
Orange Crush. I slid my dime across the counter at Bill Chew's, and he pulled a pop wet from the cooler and put it in my hand. It made me greedy. I got maybe one a week, and I wanted it all. Even the bottle was beautiful— its long skinny neck, the raised green letters you couldn't scrape away with your thumb—and worth two cents. The sun shone through the glass as I tilted the drink to my mouth. It tasted better than oranges, even the ones from Japan that came only at Christmas. There was always a kid who didn't have a dime, who wanted a sip, so I spit in the bottle, watched the bubbles slide down the neck, float on the bright liquid surface before they dissolved, and no one would drink it then, no one but me.

SPIT, v. To eject saliva from the mouth by the special effect involved in expelling saliva. (1568, Ascham, Scholem. II: Their whole knowledge... was tied onely to their tong & lips... and therefore was sone spitte out of the mouth againe.)

Five grade 1 girls played in the corner of the school grounds by the fence near the girls' entrance, just past the wide granite steps. Away from the big kids, all in a row, we grasped the wire mesh with our mittened hands, spit on the snow and then slid our feet back and forth as fast as we could to make a patch of ice. If the teacher would let us in, we'd dash through the doors down the marble floor to the fountain and fill our mouths, then dart to the fence again and splat the water at our feet. Every recess with my friends I rode the ice, frenetic as a gerbil on a wheel, my caged body running nowhere on its own spit and me too young to know what that might mean.

SPIT, 1633 P. Fletcher. *See how with streams of spit th' art drencht.*

"Come on," she said, "do it!" I gathered the saliva above my tongue, pushed it to the front of my mouth, pursed my lips and forced it out. It fell in a long translucent string, dribbled down the cheek of the girl my friend held on the ground, though the girl squirmed and started to cry. "Don't be a baby," my friend said to her. "Now you're in the club, you're one of us."

SPITTER: *One who spits. (1615, Crooke, Body of Man. Melancholy men are all of them . . . great spitters.)*

My brother hawked on the ground when I walked with him—a shocking thing—that liquid, guttural sound, then a *phhutt* to the side, right where anyone could step in bare feet or fancy shoes. He was so proud to miss his chin and jacket, to leave his mark on the cement, a circle thin and shiny as a coin, and he wasn't the only one. A chain of spit linked the squares of the sidewalk showing where the men had walked. My father and grandfather did it too, my grandfather's saliva red from snoose. Mom told my brother it was disgusting, he had to stop. "What am I supposed to do?" he said. "Swallow it?"

SPIT, 1700, Floyer, Cold Baths. Temperate bathing . . . ripens the Spit and helps it up.

The kids on the block called him Drool Face. He was the older boy who lived in the house two doors down and who never went to school. We saw him only in the summer, when he sat by the back steps on a chrome kitchen chair, his mouth open, a thin stream from the corner of his lower lip running down his chin like it did in the dentist's office until the assistant told you to spit into the bowl. Our mothers warned us to stay away from him, but one day, cutting across his yard, I came too close and he grabbed me, held me on his lap. I wasn't scared, though I knew something wasn't right. He didn't try to rub me between the legs like the old man at the paddling pool who always brought his own towel and asked to dry us. He just held me on his lap, my back against his chest, my head tucked under his chin, my legs dangling. His pants were the thick green cotton grown men wore, and his shirt had metal snap buttons down the front. I could feel them press into my back. I was glad I was turned away, because his face was hard to look at—the slack mouth and wet chin, his eyes a soft hurt brown as if he knew what people said about him. I let myself go limp in his arms and listened to his breathing. It sounded like the panting of a sick cat who had crawled under the bed and wouldn't come out. I wouldn't tell anyone. "Wally," I said, "you should let me go now," then squirmed out of his hug and ran through his yard to my friends, the top of my head damp with drool.

SPIT: *The act of spitting; an instance of this. 1658: Lovelace, Lucasta, Toad and Spider. The speckl'd Toad...Defies his foe with a fell Spit.*

My friend's brother, who was in grade 12 when I was in grade 10, took me aside at the Teen Town dance one Friday night. He was still as skinny as a little kid, and he wore a dumb-looking wool hat even though it was summer. There was something he had to tell me, but I had to promise not to get mad. It was a trick, he said, he and his friend Jimmy used to play on us. In winter they'd slobber on the branch of a tree. If it was cold enough, and they got the angle right, their saliva froze before it could hit the ground, forming a row of thin icicles. They'd wait for me and my friend to come up the alley on our way to school. "You were always giggling and chattering," he said, "we could hear you half a block away." He and Jimmy would act nice. They'd break the glass sticks from the branch and offer us the best ones, long and glittering in their hands. We'd lick the pointed ends and then put them in our mouths. Now I understood why the boys danced around us as we sucked the ice, why they laughed and punched each other in the arm, laughed so hard they doubled over and hugged themselves, hugged themselves to keep their secret from spilling out.

SPIT, sb., saliva, spittle; a clot of this. See also cuckoo-spit, frog spit.

The practical uses of human spit: To hold a kiss curl in place, to shine a shoe, to express disgust, to remove a smear of mascara, to lubricate, to seal an envelope, to slicken the lips for a photograph, to defog a scuba-diving mask, to test the hotness of an iron, to clear the throat, to turn a dull stone to jade, to determine the direction of the wind, to moisten a wad of gum or a plug of tobacco, to turn a page, to clean a face. "Wait," she would say when I was half-way out the door. "Let me look at you." Always she'd find something, lick her finger and rub at a spot on my cheek or chin. I'd wiggle free of her hands and walk from the house, marked with the snail-slide of my mother's fingers, slick tattoos telling my tribe and lineage, my face shining with the signs she drew to place me in the world.

light years

THE SUMMER we were eleven, almost every evening after supper, Lynda and I would jive in her basement to Elvis's "Don't Be Cruel." The glossy 45 spun on her portable record player, which you opened and closed with two brass snaps like the ones on a suitcase meant to travel far. When it was time to leave, I ran the four houses from Lynda's place to mine, then paused, shaking, scared to go down the six steep steps that cut through the lilac bushes leaning in on either side, the brittle hands of branches reaching out. There were no streetlights, no porch light over the door, and the curtains were closed. If I shouted no one would hear.

Sometimes Lynda snuck out her back door, sprinted ahead of me, then leapt from behind the hollyhocks and caraganas just past her house to call out, "Scaredy-cat!" My mother thought my terror came from Lynda's teasing or from the homeless men who lived in the Salvation Army house one block down, but none of them were out after the evening meal, and in the day they looked as harmless as old forgotten uncles who'd wandered off the farm and spent their hours looking for the road back to Cabri or Success or Antelope.

I didn't tell anyone the fear had arrived the first time I saw the stars, *really* saw them, looking down hard-edged and blank. When I was little, I loved to hold their gaze. Every Sunday, on our drive home from my grandparents' farm, I'd lie in the front seat with my head on Mom's lap, my feet on Dad's legs below the steering wheel. If it was winter it would be dark outside, the stars drilling their distance through the windshield and into the small place warmed by my parents and the heat blowing from the vents below the dashboard lights. One small star travelled with us in the car. It glowed round and red on the end of the lighter my dad pulled from its socket, then swept in an arc to the end of his cigarette, setting it aglow.

Then, the stars were a source of wonder as they followed us like faithful frost-quilled dogs the thirty miles from the farm to the city, where they paled slightly above the neon signs of Central Avenue. Often I'd pretend to be asleep as we pulled up to our house, and Dad would carry me from the car to my bed, the stars inside my head now, shooting luminescent needles from the dome of my skull to the bottom of my feet as Mom pulled off my boots and socks and tucked me in.

Soon I was big enough to sit alone in the back seat. Sometimes as we neared home, my skin prickled, as if I'd rolled in nettles, from the tense silence that stretched between my parents. It lasted from the car to the house and into the living room, where my father, without a word, turned on the TV. One such night, before I went to bed, I slipped outside. Lying on my back in the yard, I saw a different sky. Had someone told me the stars were dead or dying? The light that touched me was blue-white and icy, like my glowing bones as I stood on the X-ray machine at Cooper's store so the salesman and my mother could see my feet inside my new shoes. The same stars pierced the sky, but with them now came a foreboding, unnervingly familiar yet strange.

That night I knew there was no comfort in the world. Something pitiless among the stars had shown itself and seemed to know me. Among a thousand earthly things, it had picked me out for loneliness, chosen me as its cold companion, though I heard no voices and saw only stars and stars and stars, deaf and far away, staring down. I knew then that was what waited in the dark, even if the sky was clouded over or my mother in her housecoat, blind to what I feared, stood in the doorway and called me home.

the only swimmer
in the world

SWIFT CURRENT'S outdoor swimming pool was only a block and a half from our house, up the alley and past the tall dented boards of the hockey rink. I was eight when my mother started working there as a checker. The job involved hefting a wire basket full of each swimmer's clothes into a numbered position on a long, six-tiered shelf. The number was stamped on a round piece of metal clipped to an elastic band, which the swimmer stretched around an ankle. The baskets were often heavy; workers from the oil fields and construction sites arrived at the end of the day with their big boots, their clothes smelly from their labours. Mom had to dash back and forth across a concrete floor from the boys' section to the girls' as people waited for her to give them an empty basket or slapped their metal tags on the counter, impatient to change out of their dripping bathing suits.

The easier job was Mrs. Brewster's. She was the cashier. Mom got to run the register on Mrs. Brewster's days off and when Mrs. Brewster left for supper, or when Mom let her sneak home, without their supervisor knowing, to look in on her eldest son, Bobby. He was what we called retarded then. Mrs. Brewster and her husband had tried to put him in the home in Moose Jaw when he was eight, she told Mom, but he'd wailed so pitifully when they walked away that they went back and got him.

Few people knew about Bobby. During the day Mrs. Brewster left him in a room behind a baby's safety gate, though he wasn't a baby. He was around twenty, and he hadn't been expected to live that long. He couldn't talk or walk but dragged himself across the floor and wore a diaper. Mom told us Mrs. Brewster worried constantly that Bobby would be caught in a fire while she was at work or have a seizure and bang his head against the floor. She had three other kids, younger than Bobby, and perhaps one of them looked after him sometimes. Mom said she understood why Mrs. Brewster didn't hire someone to care for Bobby. She left him alone because she didn't want everyone in town to know she had a son like that. It was nobody's business but her own.

Mrs. Brewster was a friend of sorts to Mom, but she thought herself superior. Rarely would she leave her tall stool at the ticket window to help if Mom was busy. She wasn't dependent on the income from her job as Mom was, at least that's what she said, and she liked to rub it in. She claimed she cashiered because the little kids she sold tickets to made her happy, and it was nice to make some money to pay for extras, like cigarettes. Two of the fingers on her right hand were yellow like my dad's.

The Brewsters owned their house, and Mr. Brewster, who made good money as an agent at the Pioneer grain elevator, didn't drink. Even in the years when there wasn't much grain to be bought and sold, elevator agents got a cheque each month. They kept their jobs because people thought the good crops would come again next year. Unlike many local farmers, always on the verge of going under, agents could buy clothes and groceries for their families.

The first summer my mother worked at the pool, Lynda and I hung around it every day. Mom wanted me there so she could keep an eye on me. We'd line up at the window and pretend to pay, but Mom or Mrs. Brewster would let us in for free. Before we were good enough to swim laps, we'd stay in the shallow end, pinch our noses and somersault. We'd sink to the bottom and turn to face one another. Then we'd shout, the bubbles rising above our heads. When we ran out of air, we'd bob to the surface and try to figure out what the other had said. "No," Lynda would say, laughing and shaking her head, the water flying. We'd kick to the bottom and start again.

By the end of the next summer, after taking swimming lessons, I could survive in the deep end. I spent hours surface diving to the blue bottom near the grates, where everything sounded and looked different; the uncanny colour and the echoes of shouts and splashes converged to form another sense, one that had no name. The water had a body to it: it was tactile and noisy and smelled of chlorine. When you held your breath and peered up through it from the bottom to the sky, it was like looking through a sheet of broken glass, the light golden and refracted.

MOM WAS loved at the pool. She was the only mother on our block who had a job, so at first I was embarrassed, but it didn't take long before I appreciated my "in" at one of the most popular hangouts in town. All the kids knew her name, and she knew theirs. She found them funny in their little bathing suits, and as they grew older, progressing from beginners' swimming lessons to juniors', intermediates' and seniors', she enjoyed watching their flirtations, including mine. The boys cannonballed the shrieking girls as we sat around the edge, pretending to read movie magazines instead of watching them.

When I was twelve, I started work at the pool myself. I checked baskets while Mom filled in as cashier or when the pool was madly busy and a person was needed to work each side. I loved the job, because it gave me money to splurge on clothes for school. I bought good things Mom couldn't afford, like a white cardigan with pearl buttons and a small bottle of Evening in Paris perfume from the Pioneer Co-op store that had replaced Cooper's at the end of Central Avenue. By the time I was fifteen, and a lifeguard, all the corners of the pool were as familiar to me as the nooks in our house. Once I got hired to paint the girls' dressing room before the pool's opening in the spring. The new paint made the dressing room look cleaner, but nothing could help the smell. Chlorine and pee, or chlorine and Pine-Sol: I didn't know which was worse. Though the floor was swept often, it was yucky to walk across, with its swamp-like puddles of stagnant water. In the toilet stalls, soggy bits of tissue stuck to the bottom of your feet, and everywhere you trod on trails of grit brought into the changing room on people's shoes.

Perhaps because of the tricks it played on the senses, the pool was a place that deceived you into thinking no one cared where you came from. Kids from both high schools—Beatty, the school I went to at the bottom of the hill, and Irwin, the one at the top—came together in its waters, tumbled and thrashed about, then lay on the concrete, bodies glistening with the baby oil mixed with iodine we'd slathered on our skin so we'd tan the deepest brown. The hierarchy depended on how well you could swim or dive and how good you looked in a bathing suit. There, I did okay. In grades 10 and 11, one of the first girls who dared to wear a braless Speedo, I strutted around the water's edge with a lifeguard's whistle around my neck, trying to look as if I could save the drowning. Only once was I called upon to prove my worth, and luckily he was a little kid, easy to pull out. Though I'd been taught how to come at a drowning person from behind and how to break a chokehold, I wasn't sure how successful I'd be with a grown man.

There was nothing beautiful about the pool itself: it was a fenced-in concrete rectangle surrounded by a wide concrete shore, with not a tree, not a blade of grass, not a picnic table in sight. But those summers at the swimming pool were bright with parity and promise. Rich or poor, you had to put your personal belongings in a mesh basket anyone could see into, tucking your hopefully clean underwear at the bottom. You had to walk across the slimy floor of the dressing room, smell its smell, spread out your towel on bare grey cement. You basked in the sun, despaired at the screams and splashes of the little kids, walked down the apron towards the soft-drink machine as if it were a fashion runway, standing tall, holding in your stomach, hoping your ribs would show. You looked at the other girls and wished for longer legs or bigger breasts or a belly that sank as if weighed down with a stone. No one who didn't know you could have guessed the kind of house you went to after you'd retrieved your basket, donned your street clothes and walked out the dressing room door to the street, your skin reeking of chlorine.

Some nights in August, when the sun set early and the pool had closed for the evening, I'd climb the tall wire fence, drop down on the other side, remove the clothes that hid my bathing suit and slip into the eerily calm water. It was a dangerous thing to do. I'd be fired as a lifeguard if I was caught, but nothing pleased me more. Light gone from the sky, the water gleaming like a new skin, I was born again, the only swimmer in the world. I was a body in the body of the water, nameless, perfectly in place, origin unknown. I glided in a breaststroke from one end of the pool to the other and back again, barely disturbing the surface. The city around me went about its nightly business; no one knew I was there. I was on another planet, one made of a silky, liquid darkness I somehow never feared. I knew its language of lapping and languid hush, and the water, without parting, took me in.

as good as
anyone

THE YEAR I started grade 9, we moved out of our house on Fourth West because our landlady refused to fix the furnace. I wasn't happy to go. Though derelict and cold, our old place had its charms: its two storeys, its worn hardwood floors, the leaded-glass panes above the big window at the front, the oak sliding door that separated my parents' bedroom from the spacious front hall. Ever since my brother had left to play hockey—he'd been scouted by a coach for the Estevan Bruins—I'd had a bedroom of my own upstairs.

I didn't mind sharing the second floor with renters. The Andrews were gone by then, and a middle-aged couple named Mr. and Mrs. MacDonald occupied the other three rooms. They'd set up a hot plate, fridge, and chrome table and chairs in one bedroom, their bed and dresser in another, and a TV and couch in the third. Sometimes I'd check to see what they were having for supper, and if it sounded better than what my mother was cooking, I'd stay if they asked me to. The only thing I didn't like about my room was the mice I was sure I heard in the night, their paws pattering across the linoleum. Mom said there was no reason to worry: mice couldn't climb stairs. The sounds I heard must be in my head.

Our new house, half of a duplex, squatted on the corner of Herbert Street and Second Avenue East. The landlords, the Crawfords, lived across the street in a gracious two-storey painted white with green trim and shutters. He was an accountant at W.W. Smith Insurance, and ours was one of a number of rundown houses he and his wife owned and rented out. Shortly after we moved in, Mrs. Crawford invited my mother and me over for tea. She treated me like a grown-up, telling me in her thick German accent to call her Berta. Only the youngest of her three daughters joined us. The other two were at a friend's, Mrs. Crawford said, who lived on North Hill.

Everything in the room was so tidy and pretty. We each had a white napkin the size of a handkerchief, embroidered around the edge with a string of yellow daisies. While we sipped our tea and ate the ginger cookies Mrs. Crawford had made, her little girl climbed the oak frame of the living room archway with the skill and quickness of a monkey. I was impressed, but she and her sisters were too young for me to bother with.

I still had my own room, but in our new house it shared a wall with my parents' bedroom. At night, I could hear them fighting. The bathroom was below, in a dank, earth-walled cellar with low ceilings and a hanging bulb you turned on by pulling a string. A sheet of plywood that didn't reach the ceiling separated the toilet from the deep enamel tub. Alkali grew out of the cellar walls like a crystalline mould and broke through the cement on the floor that the scrap of linoleum didn't cover. Mom promised me, a fourteen-year-old sulky with the ugliness of it all, that we'd move to something better as soon as we could. Until then, I'd just have to put up with it. I snapped that I'd never invite a friend over—I'd die if anyone saw where we lived. "Tough luck," she said, and went about her tasks.

By now, my mother had a winter job too, selling tickets at the Junior A Bronco hockey games. The rink was on the outskirts of town, a couple of miles from our house. She didn't have a driver's licence and couldn't rely on my dad to show up sober or on time, so she walked through the dark and cold to the evening games. Sometimes she'd get a ride home with a fellow worker; if not, she'd make the trek on foot back again. Her small bundled figure trudged through the snow, the icy wind whipping around her. Waiting for her to arrive, I imagined watching her from high above, the only moving thing in all that white.

She and I had set off on similar walks together when I was little. Once, after we'd waited an hour for Dad to pick us up from the Eagles' Christmas party, a brown bag of hard, striped candy clutched in my hand, we plodded down the snowy streets alone. The temperature had fallen to thirty below. Halfway home, because I was shivering, she undid the big buttons on her old muskrat coat and pulled me inside, the back of my head pressing into the rise of her belly, the satin lining slipping across my forehead and nose. What strange tracks we must have printed in the snow as I blindly shuffled my feet between hers.

Besides the few bottles of beer my father kept in the garage or by the basement potato bin, there was no booze in the house. Dad did his drinking at the Legion, though he hadn't been a soldier in any war; at the Eagles' Lounge on Sunday afternoons, and at the three downtown hotels. He'd get home from work, wash his face and hands and change into a shirt and tie, then leave for a few drinks before the bars closed between five and seven. He'd return to the house to eat supper, then head out again until last call. Twice in three years he lost his driver's licence, a penalty that meant one of his fellow workers had to pick him up in the morning and drop him off at the end of their shift. Both times the judge had allowed him dispensation to drive a backhoe in the oil fields. Otherwise, he would have lost his job.

All year through, my mother did three hours a week of day work for a lawyer who lived at the top of North Hill. Taking on that job was the smartest thing she'd ever done, she said, because it showed her how the other half lived. "Let me tell you, they're no better than we are." Though she relied on her dollar-an-hour wages to buy our groceries, sometimes the lawyer's wife forgot to get money from her husband, and Mom would have to wait a week or two for her to settle up. As if to make up for this, the woman would send home clothes for me, things she'd grown tired of. Some of them were nice, more expensive than anything I owned, but they didn't suit me. I wore one of her dresses anyway, a mustard jersey shirtwaist with flat gold buttons down the front, paired with a short jacket with three-quarter-length sleeves. Though the colour wasn't flattering, I thought the outfit made me look classy.

There was one good feature of our new house—my high school was only two blocks away. That meant I could come home for lunch and wouldn't have to eat with the kids who lived south of the railroad tracks or came in from the country on buses. The school's lunchroom was nowhere you'd want to hang out, just a few rows of metal chairs in the cold, too brightly lit gymnasium.

On Friday nights, my girlfriends and boys our own age gathered at the new Country Club Café near the Lyric Theatre, where we'd order Cokes and chips with gravy. Some nights a boy would walk me home, and we'd kiss on the top step at my front door. I was too anxious to enjoy it, afraid my dad would drive up before I got inside. For a few months in grade 10, I went out with the son of a doctor. He'd already graduated from the other high school, Irwin, and was in university. His mother ran a clothing store, and he gave me a beautiful pink angora sweater for my birthday in May. It wasn't right for the season—it must have been at the bottom of the sale bin—but I couldn't wait to wear it to school in the fall. When I told Mom he'd invited me to his house for dinner, she was nervous for me. "Imagine," she said, "my daughter going to a doctor's house. Remember, you're just as good as they are." I was so uneasy at their table, trying to figure out the cutlery, that I dropped a boiled potato I was lifting from the bowl with a fork and it fell on the carpet and rolled. All of us ignored it.

High school wasn't about learning geo-trig or chemistry or Shakespeare's plays. It was about learning how to belong, how to fit in, a desperate and hopeless task. The most popular kids at Beatty weren't the smart ones but the athletes. Like my brother before me, I didn't want to be called a brain. I'd do enough cramming before tests to get good marks, but not stellar ones like Bonita Stark and Barbara Ashford, who never got asked out on a date.

Unlike my brother, I wasn't good at sports. Even if girls had played hockey, I wouldn't have been among the graceful, bladed furies streaking across the ice. I wasn't good enough for the basketball, volleyball, baseball or track teams, either. Yet I wanted to be part of something bound for glory. I wanted to go to practice and get drenched with sweat and pour water over my head to cool off. The only thing left was the cheerleading squad. Though I couldn't turn a cartwheel, I got chosen at the tryouts, maybe because the teacher advisor, Miss Bly, was also my science teacher. A few nights a week, I'd stay after school to feed the three caged gerbils and two rabbits in her classroom. Once I'd helped her lay out frogs and scalpels on the front counter for the grade 11 biology class. I couldn't wait to take that class myself and cut a frog open. Gutting the chickens on my grandparents' farm had made me hugely curious about the wonders you could find inside a body.

Dressed in a short top and flippy little skirt, I shook my pompoms with the other cheerleaders in the gym that smelled of green sawdust and sweat. We dyed our running shoes in my mother's canner to match our uniform's royal blue; she was the only mother who'd let us do that in her kitchen. Three Beach Party movies had recently played at the Lyric Theatre, with Annette Funicello and Frankie Avalon crooning and rocking in the California sun. Our skin shone fish-belly pale by the time the basketball season began in the fall, but we wanted to be as brown as Annette.

Our knees and elbows flashed orange from the Quick Tan we smeared on our skin.

I mastered the footwork of the cheerleading routines and the five jumps that concluded the yells, but I hung back when the rest of the squad cartwheeled or backflipped in front of the players' bench. It didn't take long, though, for me to find a way to make up for my lack of gymnastic skills: I became the writer of cheers. I lay in bed at night and composed words to tunes like "Long, Tall Texan," "Walk the Dog," "I Wanna Hold Your Hand" and "He's So Fine." For the "doo-lang, doo-lang, doo-lang" I substituted the name of the Beatty boys' team, accenting the last syllable: "Bar-óns, Bar-óns, Bar-óns." When I sang the cheers to myself, I was transformed into a Chiffon, a Shangri-La, a Marvellette.

During basketball season, I'd rush to practice with my verses in hand. We'd try them out, delighted to be original and risqué. We'd already lowered our voices so that we didn't squeak and shriek like the cheerleaders from Irwin. All the boys on our team had a crush on them, but we thought they sounded silly. We bought full-support bras from Woolworth's and panty girdles that stopped our flesh from jiggling when we jogged onto the court. We didn't want to be sex objects. We wanted to be taken seriously when we jumped and kicked and launched into our new repertoire in voices deep enough for a singer of the blues.

It was all going well until the captain of our team walked over after our halftime show at a tournament and told us he'd kill us if we did that shit again. "What is your point?" he asked. "Why can't you sound normal?"

LIKE MY elementary school friends, the girls I hung around with in high school took lessons my parents couldn't afford to give me. Every Sunday, one after another, they spent an hour with Mrs. Town, who taught them how to sing. After, they rehearsed in the choir she conducted, getting ready for performances at the Ladies of the Nile's strawberry tea or the United Church fall supper. My family didn't go out to the farm anymore for Sunday dinner, so my friends' lessons made the day long and lonely. Boredom seeped from every corner of the house. It settled in the yard and in the empty streets downtown. The sky was one big yawn that lasted until school began on Monday morning.

Despite my lack of training, I summoned up the courage to audition for the school operetta. Maybe it was my ululations as a cheerleader that gave me confidence in my voice. Maybe it was my mother's encouragement and her naïve, unconditional faith that my brother and I could do anything we wanted. When I failed my first swimming test and came home crying, she marched me back to the pool and signed me up for the next set of beginners' classes. When I swore I'd never learn to ride a two-wheeler, she wiped her hands on her apron, took me out to the back alley with my bike and ran alongside, holding on to the back of the seat until she finally let me go. I rolled down the gravel, the feel of her behind me, and I didn't fall off. Even if I'd taken a spill and skinned my knees, she'd have made me get up and go at it again.

Carol Baba, the school's best singer, got the lead in the operetta every year. To my surprise, the teachers holding the auditions announced I'd won the role of supporting actress; my friends were assigned to the chorus. It was my energy that impressed them, I guess, and my ability to throw myself into another character. I hadn't seen that as a strength but as a weakness; it came from pretending to the world that everything was okay in my family, that my father's drinking wasn't a secret source of shame. Now I realized I'd spent years acting. As for the singing, Mr. Brown, the teacher in charge of the musicals, said he'd show me how to talk the songs. Although he was a small, quiet man, he was known to lose his temper if a singer didn't catch on. During our practices alone in the music room, I could see he sometimes despaired, but he never banged his hands on the piano keys or bawled me out. The night of our first performance, the gym was packed. The members of the cast peeked through the curtains, trying to spot parents or schoolmates they had crushes on. I talked the songs as Mr. Brown had taught me, but whenever the choir broke in with the chorus, I'd sing with gusto, my slips in and out of key muffled by their trained, melodious voices.

The operetta was such a big event in town that the *Swift Current Sun* sent a reporter to cover the show. He wrote an article and took photographs for the next edition. My mother couldn't get over her daughter on the stage. She clipped each article in the paper—I was in the school musicals for three years running after that—and pasted them into a scrapbook she'd bought at the Co-op. On the cover was a blonde girl in a sombrero-like hat, her arms around the neck of a golden collie that looked like Lassie. Every time I saw the picture I thought of my brother being forced to take me to *Lassie Come Home* at the Lyric Theatre when I was four. I had embarrassed him in front of his friends by grabbing his hand and sobbing loudly when Lassie was lost in the pouring rain. "Shut up," he whispered, though his voice wasn't harsh. "Lassie always comes home."

My father never made it to my plays. Mom said he couldn't sit still for two hours on those metal folding chairs in the gym. What an excuse, I thought. He just didn't want to leave the shuffleboard or pool tables or give up on the Friday night meat draw at the Legion. When my mother saw the sour look on my face, she added, "There's no better man than your father when he's sober." Her tone warned me not to argue, but every time she defended him like that, I wanted to yell, "When is he sober? Why do you put up with it?" Though reporters took my picture, though I won awards at school, I was not as good as anyone. I was Emerson Crozier's daughter. That was the circle of light I stood inside no matter what I did or who I tried to be.

lonely as
a tree

BEFORE I SIGNED UP for driver training at school, my father took me out in the car a few times so I could get used to being behind the wheel. He was patient with me, though he got bored fast. He'd drive to the city limits, then stop on the shoulder where we'd change places. I'd take the car for a five-minute run on the straight stretch of highway that led north, stop at the tree, turn around and head back. The tree marked the boundary of how far my father was willing to go. It was a big cottonwood with a height of about fifty feet and a span of thirty. In another place, there would have been nothing remarkable about it, but here it was the only tree for miles.

The cottonwood was more accurately the only *wild* tree for miles, or at least the only tree that no one admitted to planting. Swift Current was summer-lush with cultivated trees in its parks and neighbourhood lots. Every farm in the surrounding countryside flaunted a shelterbelt of seasonal greenery planted in a square around the yard. Double rows of Siberian elm and caragana cut green swaths through most of the fields—not tall, gracious trees like maples or birch, but dwarfed, gnarled survivors noted for their ability to thrive on little water and to endure the heat and cold.

Provided by the government, these were humble, working trees planted to tame the wind, stopping it from blowing the topsoil away. In the years following the drought of the 1930s, each seedling was slipped into the ground by hand and watered with buckets carried from a well. If any of them on your land died from neglect, the tree inspector the next spring could make you pay. Each row of aged trees I saw when my family drove into the country, including the shelterbelt Grandpa Ford had planted in the early forties, added up to hours of hope and labour.

But not that tree. It wasn't part of any windbreak. Nor was it near a farmhouse. Its seed, embedded in soft cotton, had been carried by a bird or the wind. Its early survival might have been accidental—perhaps as an elastic sapling it had slipped between the blades that plowed the soil on either side. It's possible the farmer didn't see it until it had grown a few more inches. After that, he must have made a deliberate decision to swerve the tractor around it, allowing a rare wildness to burgeon without care at the edge of the tended field.

Besides the dapple-grey under the branches of the windbreaks, the only other shade in the fields fell from man-made things like grain sheds or giant tractor wheels. During harvest at the farm, I'd sometimes see my aunt and uncle sitting in a wheel's cool shadow eating the sandwiches she'd made, opening sealers of lemonade or iced tea beaded with water, their black-and-white collie-cross panting beside them. I had thumbed through art books in the school library, and I knew a painter could make something of that—three creatures at the centre of a dark circle, a huge machine looming over them, the sky's burning globe shedding its unremitting light. In a country without trees, you sought relief in any shadow big enough to hold you.

The cottonwood cast its shade with wide generosity. After I had passed my driver's test, Dad would sometimes give me the car for an hour or so. I'd take the road to the tree, stop on the shoulder and walk through the ditch to stand under its boughs. Its singularity and its size fascinated me. I measured out twenty-two giant strides from its trunk to the end of its shadow. So much life flourished in the area its roots and branches claimed. It was a breeding ground for robins and sparrows, its cottony seeds the perfect stuffing for a nest, the thinnest of its fallen branches scavenged by crows to build their houses of sticks. Wild grasses greened here. They were grazed by antelope and deer—I saw their rich brown droppings—the seeds a feast for birds and mice whose narrow paths tunnelled through clumps of prairie wool.

Once I stumbled upon a covey of partridges; they pulled my quickened heartbeat into the sky and out over the field until they disappeared. Grasshoppers bumped against my forehead and cheeks like fleshy pebbles some invisible bully was tossing from the long grass. On the ground over the hump where a root spread wide, I crouched to watch a darkling beetle, solitary and shiny, trundle his daily troubles away from his hole in the earth. When I looked up, the sky vanished in a green glistening of leaves that ate the light and changed it.

To the four-legged animals that populated the countryside, the tree and its pool of shade must have been a station stop, a cool watering hole without water, a pause in their journeys through the lean light of dusk and early morning. The tree was too close to the highway to be a permanent dwelling for them, but was it a landmark for foxes, coyotes, badgers? Did it say to them, *you're halfway to your sleeping den?* Did a fox rub its cheeks on the scaly bark to let others know it had been here? When I touched it, the tree touched back. I inhaled its scent and let out my breath, so small compared to the massive lungwork of its leaves.

The cottonwood was the most important landmark outside the city limits. If you heard a kid say "Let's meet at the tree" to his buddies on the first spring day they hauled their bikes out of the basement, that was the one he meant, and everyone knew it. More than one graduating class cut out paper place cards in the cottonwood's mushroom shape to set on banquet tables in the school gym. Brides and grooms had their pictures taken there. You'd see the photographs a week after the wedding in the display window of Ogilvy's Photography on Central Avenue, the tree a living backdrop to the white dresses and dark suits; the bride's veil, thin as a leaf, teased by the wind.

Long before I was old enough to drive, I'd picnicked under the tree's branches with my friends. We'd make our own sandwiches out of my mom's homemade bread and Ona's mom's chokecherry jelly. Lynda would bring three Cokes from the machine at her dad's garage. We needed those Cokes—to get to the tree we had to climb the biggest hill outside town. At least once in the summer and the early fall, we pedalled from the valley our city nested in up into the sky before the highway slightly dipped, then levelled out and rose again. Three times we would get off our bikes and push, sweat drawing the dust to our skin. Black flies BB'd our faces until we coasted in the wind down the less steep incline on the other side, hoping to go fast enough to ascend the slight rise before the tree without needing to pedal any more.

Finally there, beach towels spread and our lunch unpacked, the cottonwood's huge presence curtained us from the cars and trucks whizzing past. We were invisible, as if we were hidden in a dense forest, as if we'd opened a door and stepped into another world like kids in a story. Above our heads the leaves chattered. On a blustery day, we lay under a green river's rush and roar. Even if the wind fell still, the leaves fluttered as if sensitive to the rising and falling of our voices.

We ate the sandwiches we'd packed, drank our Cokes and touched our cheeks and foreheads to the cool, shapely bottles. If it was fall, the leaves would be as gold as the foil on chocolate coins, and we'd hear wild geese passing overhead. For reasons we didn't know then, their flight filled us with longing. Did the geese look down at us? When they saw the tree in its splendid isolation, did they measure the distance they had yet to go before the southern marshes? Beneath their wings and melancholy calls, beneath the golden branches, we knew exactly where we were. Then, we didn't know how rare that was or what it meant. We didn't know how easily you can get lost once you move away from childhood.

Sometimes we watched a storm bluster in, lightning striding from the black horizon towards our small city. If we stood tall around the trunk, our backs pressed into the rough bark, we knew we'd stay dry, at least for the few minutes before rain found its way through the loose shingles of the leaves. Sometimes a half-ton would stop, the driver loading our bikes into the back as he gave us a lecture. A tree calls the lightning down, he'd scold. His warning made the tree more magical. In our minds its branches exploded into brilliance; zigzags of silver shot down the trunk and through the roots, then burst back into the sky, the tree fusing heaven and earth with a deadly brilliant seam.

One year I drove to the tree a few days after Christmas. It had been a bad holiday—Dad out of work again, Mom weary with worry. Its branches bare, in the falling snow the tree looked lonely. I wondered if, like me, it longed for companionship, for the moon to rest on its bare shoulders, for the red-tailed hawk to preen in its highest branch. When the wind tumbled through its boughs, was the tree less alone? Did it feel a presence, warm-blooded and comforting, when an animal curled against its trunk in the night? I wondered what it made of me as I stood beneath it.

Ordinary yet remarkable, the two of us were the only upright things for miles. Beyond us on all sides, fields unrolled their bolts of white, nubbed cloth to the darkening horizon. Now that the cold had come and the leaves had fallen, the tree had stopped talking. Its branches bore the blue star-silence of the snow.

first cause: insects

flies

Surely they're the shrewdest. The ones who started it all,
needing light to pull them from the cold, warm their blood
so they could do the thing they're named for. There is
nowhere you can't find them. In outhouses on the farms
they're big as marbles and just as shiny. In the kitchens of
fancy restaurants, in garbage dumps, in pastures, in huge
cathedrals where no one blesses them, they wash their
faces before and after every meal. Their gaze is ancient and
compounded, going back before the Fathers who set down
rules in books. That buzz they make, think of it as the only
song that lasts forever, the one the whole world knows in
the darkest chamber of the heart.

grasshoppers

They come instead of rain, but they rain down, fill buckets
and troughs and flood the ground, green and slippery
underfoot. You'd think their mouths were full of teeth, so
noisy their jaws when they chew. In their leaps from place
to place there is nothing more graceful, more dolphin-like.
The farmers have laid out a feast for them across the fields.

Absent for a year or two, they return, prodigal, and there are lamentations and the pulling out of hair amidst the demented clicking of their wings. Arrogant and regal, they have been inside a pharaoh's head; they have been a pharaoh's dreams.

dragonflies

Of every insect's relationship with time, the dragonfly's is most exquisite. On Earth before the dinosaurs, the golden ones are from Byzantium, fashioned to be gilded spokes on the wheels of a machine that measures the integers of what gets lost. No matter what their colour, they're lovers in the air, the male on top clasping her neck, his long body arched and curved, and she keeps flying. Passionate, of course, yet elegant and austere. You've seen the carapaces they leave, that they crawl out of to unfold in the sun their new transparent wings to dry. Few insects are slimmer; few more eloquent. The sound they make above the slough, among the bulrushes, is like the watch of your beloved when he drapes his forearm across your shoulders and falls asleep.

miller moths

Nothing to commend them, unlike the luna or hawk or white-lined sphinx. Miller moths are the colour of dirt. The length of your thumb, they've broken off from clods of summerfallow and grown the dull, ponderous wings that heave them through the air. No one would mistake them for butterflies or angels. Gravity's insect, they seek

you out. Who knows how they get in, but they blunder
into your room, batter the window behind the blind, land
on your pillow with a small thud and crawl into your hair.
Their dust bears no resemblance to pollen or the finest flour
sifted on a pastry board. Across the wall and counterpane,
they drag their wings and leave a grimy smudge, dust with
some oil in it, close to what we must become.

mosquitoes

She gives you ample warning. Singular or in a swarm, her
insistent whine cannot be mistaken for anything else. She
makes you slap yourself hard and fast, like an angry parent
might. She shrinks your geography, limits where you walk;
every patch of grass becomes a bad neighbourhood, the
lights shot out, engines revving. At night, when you think
you are alone, her feet land among the hairs of your arm
with the lightness of an eyelash. When you feel the bite,
it's too late. Small airy thief, she has broken in, stolen what
she came for. Warm inside now, she rides the updrafts, flies
to open water where she'll lay her eggs, her need assuaged,
her promise fulfilled. You, great provider, who hoard what
you could freely give, feel only irritation and the beginning
of an itch.

ants

We should be lighting candles around their mounds;
we should be writing psalms and offering bread and sugar.
When the soil is frozen and the gravediggers can't bury
the dead, they are life continuing, sleepless in their deepest
nests below the frost line. They tunnel under your feet,

excavate chambers for their many mansions. One mind, they seem, that never stops thinking. Pulled from the dark after the thaw, pouring from the ground with particles of clay clamped between their jaws, they carry the under-world into the glare; bit by bit, without reward or glory, they recreate the Earth.

a very
personal thing

ONE OF THE BEST things about the move to our new neighbourhood, according to my mother, was that Lynda and I would be out of touch. Lynda was what Mom called "boy crazy." I knew that wasn't fair, but there was no arguing with her. Lynda had matured fast physically, and by grade 7 had started to run with her sister's crowd, two years older. In the summer between grades 8 and 9 I'd gone for a ride with her, her boyfriend, George, and George's friend. It was the closest thing to a date I'd ever had. George parked at the dam south of town, and he and Lynda slid together on the front seat and started necking. In the back, the other boy kissed me, which I liked, then touched my breast. I didn't know what to do. Lynda and I had talked about how we didn't want to be like the girls shunned by the popular kids in town. Those girls hung around the bus depot café, and most of them had dropped out of school to be carhops at the Dog 'n' Suds or to clean rooms at the motels along the highway.

Even when we were kids, boys looked at Lynda differently. Their gaze would skim over my head and rest on her, and there was a look in their eyes I had no word for. Lynda had always been tall and gangly. Our parents used to call us Mutt and Jeff; she had the legs of a colt and I, the legs of an Irish potato-digger. Often in play I'd hold my arms out to her, my hands clasped together as if in prayer, and she'd grab me by the wrists and swing me around. Sometimes she dropped me to the ground without warning and gravel studded my knees.

One afternoon soon after Lynda's eighth birthday, as we bounced her new rubber ball back and forth on the sidewalk, she told me she knew something I didn't. It happened only to women, she said, and it was happening to her right now. Her mother had made her promise not to tell me, and so she couldn't say more. At the supper table that night, I brought it up. "What did she mean?" I asked. I could tell by the silence around the table that I'd stepped into dangerous territory. My brother dug into his potatoes. My father reached for another pork chop. My mother threw me a warning look and said I should mind my own beeswax.

Four years later, when it was time for me, Mom gave me a booklet she'd ordered from Kotex called *You're a Young Lady Now*. On the cover a blonde, pigtailed girl in blue jeans gazed into her bedroom mirror; a "young lady" with her hair down and wearing a mauve party dress smiled back at her. Inside the back cover was a special 1960 calendar, where a girl, every month, could make an all-important X. Girls were advised in one caption to "Stay Neat and Sweet." That section suggested bathing once a day, something never done in my family. We'd always had renters, and there was only one bathtub to be shared among seven people. Another headline decreed, "Keep Fresh as a Daisy."

The booklet warned that even a girl's perspiration smelled stronger during that time of the month.

Though the Kotex company assured the reader menstruation was a natural part of growing up, it went on to chide, "It's a very personal thing, so you won't want to discuss it with anyone else except your mother, school nurse, or advisor." It was obvious my mother didn't want to discuss it. My only contact with the school nurse had been to line up with my classmates in the elementary school gym for booster shots for mysterious diseases, and I couldn't even imagine what an "advisor" might look like. No wonder Lynda, dying to tell me, had promised her mother not to breathe a word.

In our fifth year of elementary school—two years after Lynda had reached puberty—the Eagle Theatre began a special four o'clock double feature of rerun movies. Every Friday, Lynda and I ran from our classroom and down Central Avenue so we wouldn't be late. It was okay with our mothers as long as we stuck together and didn't stay for the second show. If they'd known some of the movies were about vampires and Frankenstein's monster, they wouldn't have let us go. On winter nights we'd run the five blocks home from streetlight to streetlight, stopping in the glowing circles and blowing out our breath visible in the cold, pretending we were smoking cigarettes in long ebony holders. If we didn't reveal our fear, we thought, the pale, hungry monsters hiding between the houses wouldn't nab us.

During a Ma and Pa Kettle movie on a May afternoon, we waited in sweet anticipation for the pigs to get drunk on Pa's moonshine, which had puddled in the barnyard after his still blew up. We were sunk in our seats a couple of rows from the front, our heads tilted back so we could see the screen, when two older boys we didn't know sat down behind us. There weren't many people in the theatre, and no one else so close to the screen. They could have sat anywhere, and when they stood up again and headed down their row to the aisle, we felt relieved. Before we could do anything, though, one pushed by Lynda and sat beside me, the other dropped into the seat next to her. We tried to get up, but the boys held us down with one hand and with the other grabbed at our chests and between our legs, laughing. I pushed my elbows into my sides so the boy leaning into me couldn't get under my T-shirt. "You're lucky you got that one," he said to his friend. "This one doesn't have any titties."

Lynda and I didn't shout or fight. Like two cornered animals, we were shocked into silence. It was the boys' laughter that brought the usher to our row with his flashlight. When he shone it on us, Lynda and I leaped up, bolted down the aisle and out the back exit. Daylight slapped our faces. We ran the block to Ham Motors, where we locked ourselves in the women's bathroom. For half an hour, we sat on the floor by the sink, then we snuck from the garage and scurried home. We knew better than to tell our mothers. We still went to the movies every Friday after school, but now we took the seats closest to the aisle, in rows near other kids. We never saw the boys again.

Lynda and I did drift apart when we started high school. It wasn't something either of us planned. But there were two sections of grade 9, and we were placed in different rooms. I'd chosen Latin and she, typing; the choice separated one group from another. On top of that, Lynda hung around with a gang of older kids who had dropped out of school. I was dating boys my own age and trying hard not to be "bad." That didn't mean I wasn't interested in sex. I felt terribly conflicted about what I wanted to do and what I *should* do in the narrow darkness of a car parked in places the streetlights didn't reach. The common spots were the dam; the gravel pit, with its hills of crushed stone; and, in spring and summer, the big parking lot behind the curling rink. No one but the most absurd romantic would have called these places lovers' lanes.

Not that it mattered. The trysts themselves were not the source of my teenage delight. The fun and sexual buzz were most delicious in the hour or so of getting ready for a date—the pink of the powder puff dusting my skin, the satiny cold cream rubbed on each toe and up my calves to the top of my thighs, the backcombing, the hairspray, the quick dab of Evening of Paris in the hollow of my neck, the tiny samples of lipstick tubes from Avon lined up on the dresser, their names full of promise: Ravishing Red, Candy Kiss, Peach Delight.

The boy who came to pick me up was never the debonair figure of my dreams. In his dad's car he'd be overly insistent and awkward, hasty and sometimes sloppily sentimental. It wasn't his eyes or hands I had preened for. No: what saved the evening were the other boys, boys whose gazes I'd catch at the movie, the Country Club Café or one of the Teen Town Friday dances, boys I knew only distantly or not at all. Among them there must be one who was waiting for me, a stranger from another town who would change my life forever.

Lynda's life changed forever much faster than mine did. In grade 10 she suddenly disappeared from school. It was generally agreed the worst thing that could happen to a girl and her family was an out-of-wedlock pregnancy. If her parents could afford it, the girl was sent to a home, though everyone pretended she was visiting an aunt in the city. When there was no extra money for room and board in Regina, Moose Jaw or Saskatoon, the girl's shame grew with her belly, if she dared to show herself in the streets.

On a cold morning in March, I saw Lynda at the drugstore, dabbing perfume on the inside of her wrist. She wore a long, baggy jacket, and she looked sad. "You've probably heard," Lynda said. "I'm not going away. I'm going to keep the baby."

No one her age in Swift Current had done that before. "Are you going to live at home?" I asked.

"No," she said. "Murray and I are going to get married next month and find our own place. My parents will help us out till he can get a better job."

You can't do that, I wanted to shout. *We're only fifteen.* But I said nothing. She and I were still the Mutt and Jeff of our childhood, and I couldn't believe how markedly she had left me behind.

In June, Lynda was forbidden to take her exams with the rest of us. When all the other students had gone, the principal sat her in a desk in the cavernous gymnasium, and she wrote the tests, one after the other. She was in her second trimester by then and had been married for two months to the big, sloppily handsome boy who was the father. The September their daughter was born, he found a job in the oil fields.

My mother felt bad for Lynda, but her fear for me pushed aside her sympathy. In the kitchen she turned from the sink and, suddenly stern, said, "You know we couldn't help you out, don't you?" Lynda's parents were lending a hand not only with the rent but with buying the baby a crib and a supply of diapers. "If you get pregnant," Mom said, "you're on your own."

Some nights after cheerleading practice, I'd walk downtown from the gym to visit Lynda at an apartment in the Christopherson Block, the same building my Grandma and Grandpa Ford now moved to in the winters, the cold and isolation of the farm finally too much for them. The red-brick, one-storey building dated from the early 1900s, and it sat across from a small mall with a drugstore, a realtor and a big SAAN that sold the cheapest clothing in town. In the hallway, I breathed in the smell of human bodies, boiled vegetables and felt-lined rubber boots warmed by radiators. Overriding everything was the sense of time turned stale, souring on the hands of the tenants and rising wearily like indoor heat to settle under the apartments' low ceilings. Lynda, her husband and the baby were the only young ones who lived in the building. Murray was rarely there, and whenever I saw him on the street, he looked cagey and sullen, even though he grinned in his old happy-go-lucky way. You knew that in a few years he'd turn to fat.

While Lynda ironed diapers in front of the TV to dry them, I bubbled with stories about the latest boy I had a crush on or the basketball tournament and its stars. I held Dani Lee, a round-faced, dark-eyed doll who rarely cried. Lynda propped the iron on its end and looked right at me. "It isn't worth it," she said. "Trust me, don't go all the way."

I didn't. No matter how much I loved the sucks and licks of pleasure or how often my body arced like a pale fish to the lure of a boy's mouth and hands, at the last minute I pulled away. Instead of my boyfriend's complaints and vows of love, I heard my friend—not what she'd told me in that shabby apartment but her voice from another time, the two of us calling to each other from the bottom of the swimming pool. When we couldn't understand what the other had said, we'd rise to the surface, take a breath and sink again, our words turning to water. How like sex it was, that going under, though we didn't know it then. In the game we played, how innocent our wet, almost naked bodies, bloodless and beyond harm.

perfect time

MOM POSED DAD and me for a photograph the night of my grade 12 graduation. I stood stiffly in my first long dress, a sleeveless, aqua *peau de soie* with small covered buttons spilling down the right side. For the first time in my life, I had a hairdo. Ginnie at the local shop had shaped my curls into a bundle of sausage rolls on top of my head. Later, I would groan every time I looked at my hair in this photo. Then I thought it was as sophisticated as anything I'd seen in a *Movietone* magazine.

Dad was wearing his only suit. It was the kind most prairie men of his background and generation saved for weddings and funerals, ignoring the shifts in fashion or their body shape. His arm was draped across my shoulders, and as he turned away from me towards the camera, his sloppy grin looked as if it was about to slide off his face. Before Mom snapped the picture, he said, "You're my little girl."

My satin high heels were dyed the same colour as my dress. Dad was in his good "oxfords," as they were called. Mel Caswell's wife had given them to him when Mel died. They were both small men with small feet, but every time Dad wore the shoes he complained they pinched. That night he'd forgotten to tie his shoelaces. After taking the picture, my mother, in a snit, sat him on the couch, yanked the laces into place and knotted a bow. He leaned on her as we walked to the door.

We were close to being late for the banquet in the school gym. We *had* to be on time; I was the valedictorian, and my family was supposed to sit with the principal at the head table, where I'd give my speech after everyone had consumed the ham, scalloped potatoes and jellied salads. Over coffee and apple pie, my fellow grads and their parents would listen to my optimistic, conservative lines about the values our elders had taught us and how these would guide us through the years to come. There was no hint of teenaged angst, no disrespect or rebellion in my speech, no true words about what I'd learned from my father. Though it was 1966, it was small-town Saskatchewan, and the sixties were happening somewhere else.

Dad hadn't come home the night before. He didn't stay away overnight all that often, but when he did we knew he'd fallen into a poker game or a heavy drinking party that didn't know how to end. "It's always when something important is happening that he acts like this," my mother said.

The last big public event in the family had been my brother's wedding two years before. The three of us had caught the night train to Winnipeg, where Barry was stationed in the air force, Dad with a bottle in his suit jacket, shouting and singing, keeping everyone awake until the porter threatened to throw him off. Shame was an everyday part of living with him, but that was the first time I willed myself to grow small, so small that no one could see me. Later, I was startled when I caught the reflection of my face in the window of the train. I thought I had made myself disappear.

The afternoon of my graduation, my mother had made me walk to the school to tell Mr. Whiteman, the teacher in charge, that my father wouldn't be at the banquet. He'd been called out of town for work, I was to say. The story was implausible, because my father's job was in the oil patch, just a few miles away. I prayed that Mr. Whiteman didn't know what Dad did for a living, and I squirmed at the thought of lying to him. He was my English teacher, I'd just gotten 97 per cent on my Easter exam, and I wanted to keep his respect. My last year of high school, I'd given up on avoiding high marks in order to fit in. I wanted to go to university, and I'd need scholarships to pay my way.

Mr. Whiteman nodded his head and said nothing as I apologized for my father's absence, but I saw something in his gaze that I'd never seen before. It wasn't disappointment or anger. Would I have known then to call it pity? Whatever it was, it made me mad, not at my parents or myself, but at my teacher. Despite the shame he caused me, the love I felt for my father was fierce. It would have been easier if I could have simply hated him.

A few hours after my meeting with Mr. Whiteman, I walked ahead of my parents to the school to relay the good news that my father was able to make it after all. The head table would need to be rearranged, my father's place card set beside mine. Trying to get to the gym before the other grads and their parents were seated, I walked as fast as I could, pounding my new thin heels so hard on the sidewalk that the rubber tip broke off my right shoe. Mr. Whiteman was standing by the stage I'd helped decorate the day before with crêpe-paper streamers, pink and aqua Kleenex roses and balloons. When I moved between the long tables across the floor towards him, one shoe made a clicking noise; the other landed without a sound. I wished anything would happen but what was about to. I wished I were any other place on Earth.

IN OUR CROWDED living room a few weeks before graduation, my father and I danced. He was good on his feet, gliding me through an old-time waltz, a two-step, a quicker foxtrot. My toes stubbed into his. No matter how many times he told me to relax, my body stiffened. At the Friday night Teen Town dances, I had no trouble with grace and daring. I twisted and jived with the best of them, and I mastered my generation's kind of waltz: my partner and I would stand almost still, swaying, arms wrapped tightly around sweaty backs as if we were keeping each other afloat. Heads bobbing in the dark, we swooned to music we barely heard above the warm rush of blood and heartbeat. But my parents' kind of dancing—the two slow, backwards steps followed by two fast ones forwards; the smooth slide through circles, the quick crossing of the floor, avoiding the couch, the chair, the big console radio—record player combination—required more coordination than I'd been born with.

My father was gentle with me; he was patient. When I could make myself relax, I followed him with a minimum of awkwardness. My feet only had to be smart enough to get us through one dance—the first of the evening, which all the grads had to endure with one of their parents. And it didn't really matter what condition Dad might be in. Drunk or not, he could make it around a dance floor without stumbling. His feet never slurred.

MY MOTHER CURLED and bowled in the afternoon ladies' leagues, and she met her neighbours for coffee once a week. But she never spoke about my father's drunkenness to anyone but me, and she warned me repeatedly not to tell my friends. His drinking was our skeleton in the closet, our mad child hidden in the attic. The bones rattled, the feet banged on the floor above our heads, but if someone else was around, we pretended not to hear. "What goes on in the family stays in the family," Mom said. "No one wants to hear your troubles."

No matter how much my father drank or how angry he became, he never hit her or me. He never abused us. She was simply covering up embarrassing behaviour, like the time he woke up in the middle of the night and peed in his shoe. Why tell anyone about that? Or the time he tripped on an imaginary branch on the sidewalk and came home with his nose scraped and bleeding and his glasses broken. Or the nights he spent in jail. She was honest and hardworking, and she wanted, in spite of our family's poverty, to hold her head up high.

In practical terms, our secret meant that I couldn't invite my friends home after school or ask them to stay for supper. I couldn't take my turn at hosting the sleepovers where my high school buddies and I danced to records in our baby-doll pyjamas, sucked back bowls of chips and cheezies, and stayed up all night talking about boys. I couldn't tell anyone the real reason Mom and I walked everywhere: Dad was too inebriated to drive, or he'd lost his licence. I couldn't tell my boyfriend why I didn't ask him to spend Christmas with my family when he was left alone, his parents responding to a relative's death a thousand miles away. What did I tell him? Another lie.

Having to lie was a burden, but the worst effect of our secret was that it forced me to hide my sadness. On the surface, I was well-adjusted, popular, optimistic. Inside I burned with shame. My father's drinking was so disgraceful that it couldn't be talked about. It had to be carried invisibly, like a terrible disease that had no name.

My father never lied about his drinking. What would be the point? But I never heard either of my parents use the word *alcoholic*. He drank, but he claimed he could hold his liquor. That ability was part of being a man, as was his right to spend his paycheque on anything he wanted. As was his prowess at arm wrestling, shuffleboard and pool. The windowsills in our living room shone with trophies he'd brought home from the bars. They competed for space with the curling trophies he and Mom had won as skips of their own teams, though that game's prizes were often more practical—matching table lamps, a big wine-coloured ottoman made out of Naugahyde, a set of cutlery, a side of beef.

For Mom, his excess stemmed from selfishness and a lack of affection for us. "He cares more about the Legion," she'd say. "He'd rather be with a bunch of drunks than with his family." But if he wasn't an alcoholic, if he could stop whenever he wanted to, the deficiencies were ours, not his. I wasn't good enough or pretty enough or smart enough to keep him home. Nor was she. He seemed to be having a good time, at least until he had to face her anger every morning before he left for work. She and I were the ones full of anxiety and despair. We were the ones sitting at home each night, dreading his arrival, hoping we'd be in bed and could pretend to be asleep when he stumbled through the door.

My father's drinking and the taboos surrounding it drew my mother and me closer together. She told me her troubles because she couldn't tell anyone else, and she became more and more independent. Sometimes she didn't keep his supper warm when he was late; sometimes she didn't tell him we'd be at a movie or a concert at the church. Once my brother had left home, it became easy to believe that she and I were the only ones who lived in the house. My father was an unwelcome, bothersome relative who dropped in from far away, demanding and unannounced. In some ways, I envied the kid I'd been when I'd wanted my father around. Now I was the one who wasn't there, flying out the front door at the honk of horn, driving around with whoever had a car, meeting the rest of my friends at the A&W and horsing around.

I HADN'T touched my father since our dancing lessons. Part of my clumsiness, my slowness to learn, had come from his sudden, unavoidable closeness. I could smell the beer on his breath, feel the occasional brush of whiskers on my cheek, the heat of his hand holding mine and the weight of his other hand in the small of my back. There had also been a surprising pleasure in being inside the circle of his arms.

During the grad banquet and my speech, my father's head nodded, and his mouth drooped open. My mother elbowed him now and then so he wouldn't pass out completely and start to snore. After the plates were cleared away, the tables folded and pushed to the sides of the gym, the band leader in his red jacket and black pants announced "the grad-parents' waltz," and my father and I walked to the centre of the floor. It was one of the valedictorian's duties to lead this dance. For a few minutes we were the only two people in the world. We were standing on an ice floe, cold and drifting, observed by hundreds of eyes. I was so afraid that something awful was about to happen, that my father would fall, that he'd say something loud about how pretty I looked and everyone would hear, that the principal would have to walk across the floor and lead us off. Everything was still. I could see my mother watching from the sidelines. Then the music started; I slid my feet to the practised steps my father had taught me. The other grads and their parents rose from their chairs and swirled around us. For a moment, I lost sight of my mother's nervous smile. I let myself go limp and moved automatically at the slightest pressure of his hands. We never spoke or stumbled. The song ended, and we had made it through as if we were normal, as if this were an easy, ordinary task. I thanked my father, walked him to my mother at the edge of the onlookers and found my date. We watched my parents dance one waltz; then, her arm in his, my mother led my father to the door to take him home.

Most of the other adults stayed for the first half of the dance, waltzing together or watching their kids' gyrations from the sidelines. I was ecstatic to be alone with my date for this special night. He was a friend, not a boyfriend, though we danced close, and later, at the wiener roast ten miles south of town, we necked in the front seat of his older brother's car. Not once in the evening did we mention my father. Not once did we say the word "drunk." I had started to believe that a glass cocoon lowered around my father after his first few beers. His loudness, his weave and stumble, the sloppiness of his smile were hidden behind the glass as long as my mother and I didn't talk about him. When we kept quiet, only we could see or hear him. To everyone else, he was invisible.

Except, perhaps, when he and I were dancing. When we glided in our best shoes across the polished gym floor, past my classmates and their parents, all of them watching, all of them thinking for the length of a song that we looked good together, this father, this daughter, moving in slow, perfect time in each other's arms.

dark water

IN THE PICTURE on my parents' bedroom wall, my mother's wedding dress, a rich, dark velvet, flowed from her shoulders to just above her ankles. Though my mother avoided sentimentality and wasn't prone to saving things with no daily use, she'd kept the dress in the back of her closet. Throughout my childhood, it was the most beautiful article of clothing in the house. On winter afternoons, I'd climb inside the closet and rub my cheek against the velvet. The dress had weight to it, and a soft, deep nap that invited you to touch and hold it like a liquid shadow in your hands.

By 1938, the year my mother and father were married, Saskatchewan had suffered eight years of drought. The fields were blowing away, there were relief lines at the CPR station, yet my mom as a young bride-to-be, with her mother, caught the train from the country to look for a gown at Kling's Ladies Wear on Railway Street. Though Mom had gone into Swift Current with her siblings and parents countless times before, this was a special journey— at twenty years old she had never owned a store-bought dress. My grandmother Ford, known for her deftness with a needle and thread, had sewn her three daughters' clothes, some of them from flour sacks, but for this occasion she'd somehow scraped together enough money, perhaps from the scarce eggs and cream produced in that dry year, to purchase a modestly priced gown. She didn't know if she and her treadle machine could handle a material fancier than they were used to, and besides, her middle daughter deserved something special.

Mom had sent home the little money she'd earned from helping her future mother-in-law do her spring cleaning and cook for the men on the threshing machine bringing in the thin fall crop. To pay for a perm, Grandma contributed a duck and a chicken Mom could sell to the Chinese café in Swift Current. The chicken died on the way, and Emerson, the man who would become my father, gave his betrothed the extra twenty-five cents she'd need to pay the hairdresser to create her curls.

Dust was blowing on my parents' wedding day. I imagined my mother running her hands over the blue-black velvet, brushing it clean in the foyer of the church before she walked down the aisle. She and Dad were going to live in a small grey shack abandoned by a homesteader. It stood across the road from his parents' farm. The reception was in their new place, and that morning she'd peeled potatoes and turnips, made stuffing for the turkey and baked three raisin pies. Her older sister had put the roaster in the wood stove just before the wedding started. Grandpa Ford had bought some beer, enough for the ten or so men who'd be crowded into the one-room shack. Just before the wedding party arrived from the church, both the bride's and the groom's younger brothers found the stash of bottles in the root cellar and downed every one. It was before my father's drinking days, so it wasn't a tragedy for him, but Mom said my grandfather was ready to take his horsewhip to their hides.

Even after I'd left for university, I'd sometimes seek out the dress on my visits home. I was relieved to find it in its old spot, unchanged and darkly beautiful. Running my hands over the spill of velvet in the closet, I pictured the guests shoulder to shoulder, wanting to brush against the bride. My mother was so gorgeous in the pictures, and I hoped she knew it for that one autumn day, because I never heard my dad or anyone but me call her pretty. Though she'd smile when I told her she was a knockout in a new pair of slacks she'd bought for curling or a Christmas sweater, I knew she didn't believe me. I thought about my father during that long-ago reception, resting his arm around her shoulders, feeling the texture of the cloth, and later sliding his hands over the rich smoothness of her hips and down her legs. The velvet, the colour of pooled ink, must have drawn the moonlight into its folds and dewlaps as it lay draped on a chair by the bed, the couple in one another's arms, their lives together stretching in front of them full of promise like the gifts they'd unwrapped earlier that day, bright with newness and good cheer in that hand-me-down, make-do time of drought and failure.

The morning after their wedding night, Mom had told me, she shook the dust out of the bedding and hung her dress on a wooden hanger on one of the nails pounded into the wall. She then caught a ride with her older brother to Success to buy a big bottle of formaldehyde from the general store. Back at her new home, in the biggest pot she could find—probably the roaster used to cook the turkey for the reception—she boiled the formaldehyde for hours on the stove. The night before, the shack had been jumping with bedbugs. The deadly home remedy killed the biting insects, and for the next few days, she and my father had to deal only with the dozens of mice that left their small hard droppings on the plates and cookie sheets and chewed the doilies Mom had embroidered for her scanty trousseau.

The velvet must have soaked up the funeral-home scent; it would have overpowered whatever perfume my mother's neck and shoulders had brushed into the fabric. By the time I buried my face in its softness, that mortuary odour was gone, and the dress had taken on the more delicate smells of time passing: traces of meals cooked on wood stoves and then electric; the musty closeness of mothballs; lilacs bursting with fragrance in the front yard; years of dust from the fields, the gravel roads and the backyard plots of potatoes. No female scent was left from the hours the dress had graced my mother's body, no smell of my father's sun-brown hands remained in the fabric, no whiff of the physical love that made my brother and then made me. I returned to the dress in the back of the closet not for its smell but for its texture, for the midnight opulence of its blue. It held the memory of my mother's young beauty, her hopeful smile in the photographs, her small flight into a life that had to be better than those hard years on the farm.

When she tried the dress on in the store, my mother told me, it was the first time she'd seen herself in a full-length mirror. Turning to the left, then the right, she stood on her toes and looked over her shoulder at the waterfall of velvet spilling down her back, almost touching the floor. She said it was like something from the movies, the watery swirl of Ginger Rogers' hem as she dipped and spun for Fred Astaire.

LIKE MY MOTHER, I was twenty when I married for the first time. By then, 1968, no bride wore anything but white. Mom and I looked for my bridal gown at the two stores in town that sold them, Christie Grant's and Yvonne's Ladies Wear. Yvonne's was considered an upscale place. When I was twelve, I'd gone there to buy Mom something for Christmas, with money I'd saved from working at the swimming pool. The owner, watching me slide the hangers along the racks to look at blouses, announced in a voice everyone could hear that I didn't belong there and should leave. I hadn't been back since.

The dress we chose was a sleeveless, straight gown with a princess waist and a long matching jacket. I thought it elegant in its simplicity, no lace, beads or ruffles. Its material was satin-like and puckered, like the surface of a pool dimpled with raindrops. Although my fiancé and I were paying for our small, no-frills wedding, like her mother my mom insisted on buying my dress. She didn't have eggs or cream to sell; she used money she'd saved from cleaning houses.

Though Mom was a spit-and-polish housekeeper, no one could make the cellar in our rented house on Herbert Street look clean, and she worried about my white dress brushing the steps and floor every time I needed the toilet. She'd arranged for me to use the Crawfords' house to change into my finery. Two hours before the wedding, I walked across the street with my dress, wrapped in tissue, draped over my arm. Mr. and Mrs. Crawford met me at the door as if I were an honoured guest. I felt comfortable with them, though my mother had mixed feelings. Ross was a hearty, friendly man, Berta was hard-working and unassuming, and though they had three daughters of their own, they'd helped me with tuition for my first year at university. They'd done it anonymously, through the school principal, but Ross soon told my mom they'd been my benefactors, lending me the $200 she didn't have. Over the years we lived across from them, they'd watched the effects of my father's drinking on Mom and me. They'd followed my high school successes in the local paper, gone to my school plays and, without saying so, concluded I was capable of rising above my station.

As landlords, the Crawfords weren't as generous. When Mom asked them to pay for a gallon of paint so she could brighten up the kitchen, or suggested that a light be installed in the cellar stairwell because she was afraid one of us would stumble in the dark and fall, they expressed anger at her temerity and refused. They ignored the gaps in the fence around the yard, the collapse of the front steps, the thinness of the insulation. It was so cold inside the house that the northern wall in my bedroom was furred with frost on winter mornings.

Standing on the pale carpet in the Crawfords' upstairs guest room, I stared at my tall, chic self in the mirror on the closet door. The straight lines of my dress and the bun on top of my head that tamed my curls added inches to my five-foot-three frame. The dress was pristine and cool, as if the fabric had been cut from newly fallen snow. I wore white satin shoes and the string of cultured pearls my fiancé had given me the night before. He was a working-class kid like me, and I knew he'd chosen the most refined thing he could imagine. They'd come in a black velvet box shaped like a flattened scallop shell, and a tiny diamond chip shone in the centre of the clasp.

No one looking at me would have said I didn't belong in this fancy house, this large, sun-filled room with its tulle curtains and pale-yellow bedspread with four, not two, pillows, an abundance I'd never seen. I floated pearled, pale and untouchable down the hall to the gleaming bathroom, turned a glass doorknob and stood in front of the three-sided mirror above the sink. There were matching white towels and washcloths by the tub and pink roses from the garden on the counter. The soap in its own little dish was shaped like a fully opened rose. I knew Mrs. Crawford had done her best to make her house pretty on my wedding day. I bent to smell the blossoms. For reasons I didn't understand, the beauty made me feel like weeping, as if I'd inhaled the thorns, not the perfume. I was trying so hard to escape who I was and where I'd come from, to love the man I'd chosen with all my heart. I wanted to fit in, to do what all my friends were doing, to be a "good girl," not a fallen one.

One reason I was getting married was to break my maidenly state: I was tired of saying "no." My mother was relieved. She wouldn't have to worry about an unwed daughter's pregnancy any more, and she could see that the honour-roll young man I'd met at university had two things strongly in his favour: he wasn't a drinker, and he had a steady job teaching high school math and physics.

Walking down the aisle in my white gown, I knew I was doing something wrong, something untrue to myself, though I couldn't have said who that self was or would turn out to be. My husband was a good man, and it would take me ten years to learn the last thing I wanted then was goodness. I wanted sparks and conflagration. I wanted to strike big wooden matches and burn my fingers. If I'd bought a dress to leave that marriage, it would have been bright red with a wide skirt that swished and swirled as I strode away.

Sometime in my late twenties, I called to ask Mom if I could wear her dress to an art gallery opening. She'd cut it up for cushion covers, she told me. I was stunned, even more so when I saw the cushions. She hadn't taken the time to sew a smooth seam in the covers, and rather than buy proper stuffing she'd bent and folded two old pillows into the corners. The cushions were lumpy and their colour didn't match anything in the room. Was she simply being thrifty? Was she sick of her dress and what it stood for?

I was never able to remember what I did with my own wedding dress. Surely I didn't leave it behind in the blue metal trunk Mom bought me when I turned eighteen and moved from home to go to university. Surely it didn't sit in the basement of the house I'd owned with my husband, waiting for him and his new wife to find it. He'd met her at the high school where he and I both once worked. She taught home economics and designed and sewed her gown by hand. People said it was a masterpiece, nothing like it in the stores.

My husband did one thing that made my parents partly understand why I'd had to leave him. In August, ten summers after that day in the Crawford guest room, I packed up my car and headed down the road to Winnipeg to be with Patrick, the man I'd later marry. At the end of September, my parents drove out to the acreage where my first husband still lived. They'd come to dig up the potatoes we'd let them plant that spring. It was a huge plot of earth, and as they pulled up to it in their car, they saw that the whole thing had been rototilled, the potatoes split into small pieces by the spinning blades. There was nothing left to harvest. For two farm people who'd survived the years of drought, there couldn't have been a surer sign of bad character.

If it's true that our spirits exist pre-birth in some kind of ether, looking down, I'm sure I chose my mother when I saw her in that dress, the material so plush it briefly held the strokes of fingers. In spite of the harshness of the setting, the failed crops and dust, I picked the prairies as my home because she lived there; I opened my eyes to the startling light pouring around her as she stood on the church's top step. Just before she walked through the door to stand by my father, did she look up and meet my gaze? Did she sense me then and draw me to her? From the day of her wedding, I waited for my time to live inside her, the velvet she had chosen the same colour as the dark water that would hold me ten years later in her womb.

first cause: grass

COME TO LIFE each spring, who knows more about being born again? Grass rolls on the earth, thrashes in the wind, speaks in tongues thin as a hummingbird's. Blue-eyed, Little Quaking, Prairie Wool, Brome. Grass could be Appalachian. In its country churches without doors and windows, without roofs, it charms the snakes. Limbless, they rasp through the stems. They belly-glide; then, sleepy as cats, they draw circle after circle and lie still. Lovers, too, recline in the meadow, believing grass douses their bright flare so no one can see them. In ditches and unscythed lots, children duck and whisper, hiding from the one who counts to ten. Prairie Satin, Fox Sedge, Wild Rye. You are grass's daughter, grass's son. It will never orphan you. Even as you wade through the lush creases of a coulee, burs and spears catching in your socks, it knots and thatches, becoming day by day the blanket that will warm you when you sink into the earth. Foul Manna, Needle Grass, Dropseed, Switch.

first cause: gravel

BLUNT MATTER, unambiguous. On its surface, no moss
or lichen grows. Sun and rain can't make it glitter, nor
wind coax it into music. Among its countless small, grey
pieces, none are asking to be saved.

You can think of nothing more speechless yet less
in need of speech, its inflections so flatly clear. There's no
un-man-made, earthly thing more lifeless. So much of it,
it's easy to forget once it was a mountain. Though you're
on the level, on the grid, you're climbing cliffs of fall.

Nothing so resists pathetic fallacies. But being human,
heading out alone, you can't ignore how it pulls like tides
under tires, shifts and slides, seems unsettled. Hauled
by truck from somewhere else, its need-to-go tremors
the road, moving you as you move, neither of you able to
return to where you started from.

What can you know of anything so unlike yourself,
without eyes or feet, without a drop of liquid in what
cannot be mistaken for a shell? It defies comparison or care.
Say only it is commonplace, and everywhere a prairie road
can go.

first cause: horizon

IF YOU could get remotely close, you'd shake like someone
with St. Vitus, the energy so intense where sky slams into
earth you'd burst into a dancing fire. There, the folios of
Galileo disintegrate to ash: the horizon convinces you the
Earth is flat. You watch the sun rise, arch across the sky.
In the evening, you spin a semicircle to watch it fall. You
walk and walk towards that straight line. It recedes, though
nothing is more still or bears more resemblance to a desti-
nation, a meeting place where suitcases sit in a row across
a marble floor, and passengers, with bare open faces, look
for someone they once loved. Certain times of day, a freight
train turns the horizon into something solid. Cars shift
quickly from east to west, no bend or curve to snag the
noisy zipper of wheels on steel tracks. You don't know if
the horizon marks the end of earth and sky or their beginning, or if one rises from the other's death like luminescent
bees lifting from a badger's shallow skull. Still, you try to
get there. Every year, you're convinced you're closer than
you were before.

the diamond ring

EARLY ONE Sunday morning, my father called me in Saskatoon, where Patrick and I had been living for the past few years. At first I was afraid that something had happened to Mom—he never phoned me. "No," he said, "she's okay, she's gone to church. I just need you to do something."

The something he needed me to do turned out to be finding a jeweller in the city who would appraise a diamond ring. A diamond ring? He didn't own one. "Why don't you take it to Fowne's Jewellers in Swift Current?" I asked. "He's as good as anyone I can find here."

There was a pause on the line, then, "I don't want anyone to know."

My father had always had his eye out for a deal. Mom and I thought he'd have made a good junk dealer like Mr. Froese, who started out storing what looked like scraps and trash in his barn at the edge of town, then opened his own business and ended up rich. Dad loved nothing better than buying something cheap and selling it for a profit. Even my mother and I couldn't escape his innate delight in bargaining. If I wanted to go to a movie, for instance, he wouldn't give me what it cost outright. He'd start with a third of what I needed and force me to cajole and humour him, nickel by nickel, until I had the full twenty-five cents. Mom had to do the same thing when she asked for grocery money.

One of the best places to make a deal, shady or not, was in the local bars. Dad would come home with items like a fancy set of steak knives with horn handles, telling Mom they'd fallen off the back of a truck. The guy who'd sold them to my father just happened to be walking by as the truck rounded the corner. His most serious thievery was several yards of thin steel pipe he brought home from the oil fields and hid in the long crabgrass in our backyard. For weeks, Mom and I feared the police would show up at our door. "They were just sitting out there," he told us. "It's not a crime to pick up something laying in the open."

I had tried to explain the buyer-beware side of my father's character to Patrick, but somehow my warnings had missed the mark. In the early eighties, when I was a writer-in-residence at the local community college for a year, the two of us rented a house in Swift Current. Patrick asked Dad if he could find him a bargain on a second-hand car. It didn't take long for Dad to show up with a dirty-brown Ford, about eighteen years old, with a cracked dashboard and torn upholstery, the sponge padding pushing through. "She may not look so good, but she's got a good motor," Dad said, "and the guy'll let you have her for four hundred bucks." Patrick thought it a fair price and went to the bank so he could pay my dad in cash. We soon found out that the car burned oil, its muffler roared and rain leaked in from the upper top right of the driver's windshield. There was worse, however, to come.

I'd told Mom the cost of the car, and a couple of weeks later, she appeared at our door with money in her hand. She'd learned that my father had paid the former owner, one of his drinking buddies at the Legion, only $200. She insisted that Patrick take the difference from her. He was shocked. In his large family, no one would ever cheat an in-law. Mom and I weren't surprised. "It isn't personal," I said. "It's just my father." Without an ounce of guilt, Dad would have delighted in badgering the seller down, upping the price for Patrick and pocketing the profit as his commission. So what if he hadn't told the whole story? It was money well earned. Patrick didn't know how to barter—he'd have paid top dollar anyway—and the car wasn't so bad, was it? Everyone was a winner.

Now we had to contend with my father's strange phone call and something about a diamond ring. Where had he got it? I wondered. Was he finally going to be arrested? "Mom and I'll drive to Saskatoon next weekend, okay? You have someone lined up. And don't say anything to her. We're just coming to see you."

There was no way my mother would believe a visit initiated by my father didn't have an ulterior motive. He was a terrible guest. He'd start fidgeting and biting his nails before he even stepped in the door. Our house was too cold for him, we ate too late—sometimes near six o'clock—we wouldn't watch wrestling on TV, and he never liked the food I put on the table. Then there'd be the sitting around trying to carry on a conversation. He rarely had anything to say. And when we were all there, in the same room, everyone noted how many beers he'd drunk.

By the time my parents had made the three-hour drive to Saskatoon, Mom had wheedled the story out of him and wanted nothing to do with it. She didn't want me to get involved, either. Patrick, still not understanding my father, agreed to take him to the appraiser I'd found in the Yellow Pages. But he'd only do it if Dad filled us in before they left.

My father had always been a superior athlete. When he was a kid he pitched softball to win district tournaments, and he'd raced horses at the rural sports days. After he and Mom moved to town, both of them became champion curlers. Even half-cut, my father would almost always win. He'd grin as he walked into the house after the yearly bonspiel, carrying trophies and lamps, copper-pounded pictures, plastic TV tables, a chrome kitchen suite or a box of frozen beef. Once he won a quarter of a car. When he phoned from Lloydminster to tell us, Mom and I jumped up and down on their bed, holding hands and screaming. Nothing that wonderful had ever happened to us.

The eye-and-hand coordination that made my father a champion on the ice transferred to the pool tables in the pubs. Few could beat him. It seemed to make sense, then, when he suggested to the Legion that he buy their two pool tables. They'd been thinking of moving the tables out. No one wanted to take care of them, and the green felt was getting shabby. In exchange for the money he collected for the games, Dad agreed to give the Legion 10 per cent of the take and keep the felts and cues in good condition. Every

Saturday morning, before the bar opened for business, he went in to empty the metal coin boxes, clean the tables and brush the felt. A few days before his phone call to me, he'd found a man's diamond ring tucked in the bottom of one of the pockets.

"Ask him if he knows who it belongs to," my mother said in the kitchen as she unpacked the loaves of bread she had baked and brought from Swift Current.

"Will you get off my back!"

Dad did know. He'd seen the ring on the hand of a loud-mouthed cattle buyer who'd stop in Swift Current on his regular rounds for one of Medicine Hat's meat-packing plants. Because he wasn't a local, keeping the ring, at least until Dad could figure out its value, seemed reasonable. Besides, the man had never mentioned he'd lost it, and he was a braggart, always exclaiming that Alberta was better than Saskatchewan. On top of that, he was a poor loser. He'd look right at Dad and complain about the lie of the pool tables, and he'd never buy the winner a beer.

While Mom and I started supper, Patrick drove Dad to a little jewellery store on the seedy side of Twentieth Street, an area where I thought few questions would be asked. On the phone, the owner had seemed competent but not suspicious. He said he'd been in the business for fifty years and knew what things were worth. I had no idea how to handle what could be called "hot stuff." This was the best I could do.

Dad was sure the ring was worth a couple of thousand at least. Several small stones surrounded the one in the middle, which was the size of a kernel of corn. Dad had asked

Patrick to take him to the store just before closing, when no other customers would be around. Once inside, my father, a cross between cocky and sly, walked right up to the man in the back who was working on a watch, a magnifying glass pinched over one eye. With no explanation, Dad plunked the ring on the table. The watch repairman must have been the owner; he was an older, weary-looking man, Patrick said, and he was alone.

"What could a guy get for a ring like this?" Dad said, acting casual.

It took only a minute or two for the reply. "Two hundred bucks," the man said. Patrick told me later that Dad looked as if someone had farted in the room. "The stones are of poor quality, and they're smaller than they look."

"C'mon," my father said, "look again."

"Not interested."

Back on the street, Dad's face was flushed with fury. "That guy doesn't know shit from tar," he said. No one was going to jew him, he told Patrick. He was smarter than that. The old bugger was a cheat and a fraud. It was too late to try another store, so Patrick sought out a bar with a pool table to distract him.

I knew that my father would blame his son-in-law for the failure of whatever scheme he'd had in mind. There was an obvious flaw in Patrick's character—he didn't know how to be the straight man in an important negotiation; he didn't know how to find a fence who knew the value of diamonds and was willing to give and take a little. Would my father have sold the ring and pocketed the money if the price had matched the figure in his imagination? Or was he just curious, as he'd have had us believe, wanting to determine the magnitude of the favour he'd be granting when he gave the ring back?

About a week later, Mom phoned for our regular Sunday chat. When I brought up the ring she told me Dad had returned it. In front of the Legion regulars, he'd pulled the ring out of a pool-table pocket. "Well, I'll be go-to-hell!" he said. When the cattle buyer dropped by after an auction in the middle of the week, my father the hero let him in on the good news. "I've got something here you might like to take a look at." He uncurled his fist, the ring shining in his palm. Dad announced where he'd found it, and the cattle buyer snatched it from his hand as if it were about to disappear again. Dad told Mom the big Albertan spat out a thank you, then said he'd lost the ring over a week ago. Wasn't it odd it hadn't turned up until now?

The man didn't offer Dad a reward, didn't even buy him a drink. "He's a goddam skinflint," Dad said. "I wish I'd smashed that shitty piece of glass with an eight ball."

My last encounter with the parsimonious side of my father's character would take place four years later, around his deathbed. His most prized possession was a 1972 bronze El Camino, a strange mutation of a vehicle, half car, half truck. I'd caught the bus from Saskatoon to sit with him and Mom in the hospital, and I planned to go back the same way a few days later. She suggested I take the El Camino. Dad wouldn't need it any more, and it would save me time. All that day, Dad had been quiet; in fact, I'd wondered how much of my mom's and my conversation he'd been able to hear, let alone understand. Suddenly he sat straight up in bed. "Whose truck is it?" he asked and glared at me and Mom. They were the last words he spoke to me.

"Yours," I said. "Dad, it's yours."

The El Camino was the only thing of my father's I inherited. Patrick and I drove it for about five years, until the bottom floor on the passenger's side had rusted through and we could see the road spinning past underneath us. We sold it to a neighbour who wanted to use it to haul his garden waste to the dump. We liked him, so we accepted his offer with no dickering. He sold the truck for double the price about six months later to the teacher who ran the autobody shop at the local school. With the help of his students he was going to restore the El Camino and make it vintage.

Dad had been right—there was a weakness in our characters. We had no guts, no skill, no delight in the bargainer's thrust and parry; we let people take advantage. If he'd heard what we'd been paid for the truck he'd refused to sell, he'd have been disgusted. We didn't know what things were worth.

till death do
us part

LONG BEFORE DAD became ill with lymphoma, my mother insisted he tell us what he wanted done with his body when he died. She'd expressed her own wishes to me, and in her pragmatic way, she wanted Dad to figure out his while he still had his druthers. I was home for a visit when she raised the topic, and the three of us were watching the hockey game on TV. My parents were living in a decent house by then. Grandpa Ford had bought it a decade earlier for $6,000, and Mom and Dad gave him $50 a month until they'd paid it off.

I wasn't prepared for the discussion, but there was no stopping my mother once she got going. "Tell Lorna while she's here," she said, "and while you're not in a coma or anything."

Dad looked as taken aback as I felt. He kept staring at the TV, though hockey wasn't really his thing. He preferred world wrestling or baseball. "I don't know," he finally said.

"Well, I'm going to be cremated. Do you want that too?" Dad said nothing. "There's no sense in buying plots—that's just a waste of money. Besides, with the kids so far away there'll be no one here to take care of them."

"I guess that would be okay, to be cremated."

"What should we do with your ashes?"

There was another pause, as Guy Lafleur scored a goal against Toronto. A minute later, Wendel Clark got a penalty for elbowing. "You could hire a plane," Dad said, "and drop the ashes over the roof of the house."

My father loved planes. In the mid-1940s, as the war was coming to an end, he'd gotten a job driving the flight crews to Swift Current's small airstrip on the edge of town. Decades later, my brother ended up in the air force, flying search-and-rescue helicopters over the Atlantic and the North. Every time a helicopter went over their house, my parents would stand in the yard and wave, in case it was my brother somehow wired like a homing pigeon and heading west.

"That's just like you," Mom said, "to come up with something expensive. We can't afford a plane. Besides, I don't want you hanging over my head on the roof for the rest of my life!"

Dad looked confused. He sipped at his beer, the organ in Maple Leaf Gardens blasting out its maddened song.

"What about the garden?" I asked.

"That's a good idea," he said. "You could dump me in the garden."

"No way. I'd be tasting you every time I ate a potato." Mom turned to me, and then, with a mischievous look, said, "Maybe we could pour him in an empty beer bottle, pop a cork in it and throw it in Duncairn Dam."

"That wouldn't be a bad idea," Dad said. Relieved at his response, I laughed. He and Mom did too.

Duncairn Dam was a good choice. During my summer holidays before high school, Dad and I went fishing almost every Sunday afternoon at the dam in his speedboat while Mom worked at the swimming pool. The first day he'd pulled the boat into our backyard on Fourth West, Mom was furious. There was barely enough to make the rent or buy groceries, yet he'd bought a boat. We didn't know where he'd found the money, but his pockets were bottomless when there was something he wanted.

At Duncairn, Dad would drink three or four beers, tipping the empties over the gunwales to fill them with water, then letting them sink. "Don't tell Mom," he'd say, and I never did. We'd go home to the chicken she had fried in case we didn't catch any fish, our faces red from wind and sun. I'd always say I'd had a good time.

I didn't let Mom know I felt lonely and bored in the boat with my father—I could never take a friend because I didn't know what kind of condition he'd be in, and he and I didn't find it easy to talk. The usual routine was to roar back and forth across the water several times, sit fishing for what seemed like days, then zoom from one end of the dam to the other until the motor was almost out of gas. At last we'd putter in to shore, where Dad loaded the boat onto the trailer and we'd start the forty-or-so-mile drive home. Sometimes I'd get to water-ski if it wasn't too windy. Our game was that he'd try to dump me, yanking the steering wheel rapidly to the left, then the right. It was a source of pride for him when I stayed upright, banging over the hard, bumpy wake, skis rat-a-tat-tatting like a machine gun in a gangster movie. I loved the noise, the ferocious rush of the wind and my father's head turning to look back at me while I swung from side to side like a crazed pendulum, almost lifting off into the sky.

My parents' faces flickered in the fiery action of the game on the screen.

"Where are you going to be?" he asked, and looked at Mom. "I think I want to be with you."

I waited for her to say something like, "That'd be a first." Or, "You want to be with me when you're dead? You never spend any time with me now." But she didn't lash out. Instead she got quiet, and the hockey game suddenly became interesting again. I let my eyes rest on the lamp on top of the TV. Although the brand of the television had changed over the years, from a wood-encased Fleetwood to an RCA to a Hitachi, the lamp had been there since Dad brought home our first set the year I was eight. It was a square piece of plastic with a light bulb behind. When it was turned on you saw a cowboy in silhouette, riding a horse, with an orange-and-yellow sunset blazing behind him and a dog trotting alongside.

After we watched the Leafs kill their latest penalty, Mom told Dad she wanted her ashes scattered on the farm where she grew up, by the freshwater stream that ran into the lake. "You remember where that is," she said to him, "the green spot just beyond the quicksand where the cow went under." She'd told me she thought it was as good a place as any.

"That's it, then," Dad said. "I'll go there too."

"And I don't want a funeral," she added. "Just the family. They can sing 'How Great Thou Art' by the lake, and someone can read the Twenty-third Psalm."

"Okay by me."

"Well, that's that," Mom said. "Lorna, let your brother know."

We scattered my father's ashes by the lake on a cold day in spring, the ground wet and slippery under our shoes. It was an alkali lake, thick with salt, encrusted with a white scab around its shores and exuding a rotting, brooding fecundity. It nestled in what could have been a pretty setting, at the bottom of hills prickly with cacti and spackled with lichened stones, but Uncle Lyn had turned the crest of the hill closest to the house into a garbage dump. It was strewn with old washers and stoves, oil barrels, the husks of cars, phantom combines waiting for a phantom crop. Down the slope, years of my uncle's rye whiskey bottles glinted in the sun, some broken, others intact, labels peeled away by rain and snow.

It was the only lake for miles around when my mother was a child, and it was all she knew of beauty. Aspens spilled out of the coulee's tucks and folds and cooled the summer days with noisy shade. Mallard ducks, unbothered by the stench or the taste, bobbed up and down on the wind-pleated water. Though the raw salt starched her hair and coated her face in a thin, stiff mask, she swam there every summer until she married and left home. The alkali-dense water made her buoyant.

My parents had worked out these last rites in less time than it took for a power play in a hockey game. Of course, they had grown up on farms across the road from one another. They'd known each other as children. The minerals leaching into the food and water that nourished them came from the same dry wheatland soil. They listened to the same wind, the same bird calls, the daily sibilance of the grass. Their eyes filled with the unblinking prairie light that candled the stubble at dawn.

At the lake, my mother scooped out a handful of ashes and released the last of my father to the wind. "There you go, Emerson," she said. She dusted her hands on her dress. "You made my life better." It was one of the most shocking things I'd ever heard. Only she knew what he had given her; only she could offer him those final words of love and praise.

my mother for
a long time

AUNTIE GLAD lived across the street in a bungalow that could have been the twin of my mother's. The same white siding, the same slope to the roof, the same narrow verandah. At ninety-five, she was the eldest in their family, and of seven siblings, she would be the last one left. Like my mother, Glad was severely independent, living alone since her husband had died over thirty years before. Recently, though, she'd begun losing track of time. The day of the week, the year, even the seasons seemed to slide into one another like water pouring from the pump into a half-full pail.

During my aunt's years of canning and preserving, on the labels of her jars of fruit, jams and jellies, she'd note in pen and ink a significant happening from the day. On the glass jar glowing a burgundy-red in her cupboard, the label said, "August 12, 1999, Chokecherry Jelly. Frieda Fitch broke her hip." On a taller jar of saskatoons on her cellar shelf, she'd printed, "July 21, 1980. Jock MacPherson died in bed," and on a stubby sealer, brown inside, "September 8, 1972. Mincemeat. Russia 5, Canada 3." She'd also kept journals over the years, starting in 1932 when she was a young woman. Most of the entries were as brief as her labels, the thin books full of the weather and simple daily tasks. "Went to the Yuricks for water today. Stopped for coffee." Or, "Hens not laying. One egg this week. Rusty and I played crib for it." Or, "Had a bath," an event important enough to record every time. In the journal for 1948, on May 24 she wrote, "Peggy had a baby girl"—those five words alone on the page, no other entry for the rest of the year about the newest member of the family. I was that baby. My aunt's unadorned notation marked the written beginning of my long relationship with her, with my mother and with words.

HOW CLEARLY the scene unwound, burned into the oldest part of my brain. Going down the wooden steps into our dirt cellar (was I four?) to get a jar of pickles. The descent came back detail by detail—my little-girl shoes, the sundress I wore out to play, my hand clutching the smooth railing. I had to be careful; there was a gap between each step where the dark poured out. The cellar was an open mouth dug into the earth. Outside, there was a small wooden door you could lift if you were as big as my brother and crawl inside and no one would ever find you.

Alkali grew through the cellar's damp walls like a poisonous white mould. And the smells were funny there. Something sweet, something rotten, something growing. The bare light bulb burned above me, its long string hanging just within my reach. Water made noises in the cistern even when it wasn't raining and nothing inside its tin walls should have been moving. I was sure I heard the lapping of waves, as if a blunt, fishlike creature had surfaced and was blindly swimming for the light.

To get the pickles, I had to walk across the dirt floor on the sheet of cracked linoleum, past the bin where potatoes stretched their thin arms through the slats to pull you in. The only good thing was the shelves loaded with preserves, the crabapples and saskatoons casting their own soft glow, ripe sun trapped inside glass. I was on my toes, my hand reaching for the jar, when suddenly I heard a scuffle near the bin. A lizard scuttled from the dark, then stopped in the middle of the floor and stared. I ran to the steps and screamed for Mom. Down she came, apron flapping, a butcher knife in her hand. She stepped on the lizard's tail, stabbed it in the back, opened the furnace door and threw it in. How fierce she was, how strong! This is my first memory, I told Patrick, the first picture of my mother. All my life I've carried this image of her bravery, her lack of hesitation, the strange blood on her hands.

"But Lorna," Patrick said, "it wouldn't have been a lizard. They aren't any in Saskatchewan. It was probably a salamander. Remember you were four and it would've looked big to you. Your memory's playing tricks."

How I argued for memory, the green body writhing on the knife, the boldness of my mother's hands, the flames dancing on the black door of the coal furnace as she swung it open on its big hinges and slammed it shut. A lizard. At least a foot long.

"Phone your mother," Patrick said. "Ask her how big it was."

I dialled the number I'd been dialling all my life. "Mom," I said, "remember that time in the cellar? You stabbed a lizard in the back and threw it in the furnace?"

"What are you talking about?" she said. "You must've been dreaming. I never would've done that."

Her response stunned me into silence.

She must have forgotten, I thought, or her battle with the dragon was so frightening she'd had to bury it deep in her mind where she couldn't call it back. Nothing I said on the phone convinced her.

"You were always such an imaginative child," she said.

That scene in the cellar, as much as anything in my childhood, shaped how I saw my mother—her courage, her invincibility. Years later I came across a passage from the Talmud. If I'd known it then, it might have made me feel better when she insisted I'd been dreaming. I could have replied, "I am yours and my dreams are yours. I have dreamed a dream and I do not know what it means."

THE MAY of her eighty-eighth birthday, my mother was not strong enough to clean her windows. By July she couldn't pick her peas or dig potatoes, though only two months earlier she'd planted a garden huge enough for two big combines to park side by side. I thought a good death for her would be to fall between the rows; when she didn't answer the phone that day, a friend would find her among the tall peas. She was not strong enough to walk the half block to the park as she had done the week before, leaning into me, not strong enough to make her meals or to pull the wide blue blinds down in the morning in the verandah to keep out the sun. One day she told me she couldn't dress herself. She perched on the edge of the bed, and I asked her to raise her bum so I could pull on her underwear, then the summer shorts she'd chosen for the heat. She didn't need to tell me she was strong enough to die. I could see it in her face, in the brown hand that clawed my forearm when she pulled herself slowly to her feet. She was not just getting off the bed but starting her difficult climb, rung by rung, up the invisible ladder to the sun.

ONE REASON she was ready to go, my mother said, was that she could finally leave her sister Glad behind. What a relief! Glad had been a burden since she'd moved in across the street, Mom having to do her bills, mail her letters, buy her groceries and sometimes cook her meals. That April, even though my mother's illness had sapped her of energy, she'd done Glad's spring cleaning after she'd finished her own. And Glad was never appreciative. All their lives she'd found fault with my mother, and she'd carried her nastiness from childhood into their adult relationship. I kept telling Mom that she was too old to take care of her sister, but Glad was in her nineties, she said, and her mind was going. Over the last few years she'd had a number of ministrokes. My mother had to remind her to go to the doctor, to see her hairdresser for her weekly shampoo, to put her meat in the fridge and throw away the moulding leftovers. People kept stealing from her, Glad told my mother: money from her wallet, an old rubber garden hose, her hearing aid and glasses, one day a sheet of oatmeal cookies she hadn't baked. Mom said her sister had always surmised things. Childless, Glad explained to the hairdresser that her mother had sewed her up when she turned eleven, stitched her shut with a long red thread. The gypsies showed her mother how to do it. "Grandma was a good sewer," Mom said to me, "but she didn't do *that*." Glad's husband was sterile because he'd had the mumps. The town doctor had warned her of the problem before the wedding and advised her to back out before it was too late.

When they were kids, Glad kept her siblings under control with a horsewhip and tattled to their strict father when he came in from the fields for supper. Because of her snitching, usually one of them, though the meal was sparse, had to go without the rice pudding Grandma made for dessert every day of the week. Not even any raisins in it, just white rice and milk with cinnamon sprinkled on the top. Grandma baked it in the oven in the big enamel pan they used later to wash the dishes and, once a week, to wash their hair.

"WHEN I SEE your dad again," Mom said, "we're going to go skating." So far, that was the most astonishing thing she'd said about her readiness to go. After all they'd been through, after all the difficulties his drinking and selfishness had caused, that was what she saw them doing when they met sixteen years after his death. I caught a sob in my throat when she told me that. When she saw Dad again, they were going skating.

MY MOTHER never spoke badly of her parents. Her silence was a pact she'd signed in blood, like many of her generation. No use complaining; there were worse off than you. She'd told me about being sent at five to the farm down the road, to live with the Winstons. For the next ten years, she was their slave child.

One of her tasks was to pull weeds from the field where the Winstons had planted their crop. When we drove near Success one August, my mother pointed at the yellow flowers in the ditch. "See," she said, "they're sunflowers and they grow in the gumbo."

"I think they're brown-eyed Susans, Mom."

"I don't care what you call them. I hate them, they're what I had to pull out day after day in the heat." I'd never heard that detail of her story before.

There's a photo of my mother around age six with her siblings and her parents. It must have been taken one of the times she was allowed back home. Behind them, the dust settles just for the time it takes the camera to catch the scene and its gawky, bird-boned children. Her hair's "straight as a board," her dress shapeless. She has no shoes, same as her brothers and sisters, and she doesn't smile. She never smiles in any photograph taken of her and her family.

"I must learn a new way of weeping," the Peruvian poet César Vallejo wrote. For now, I thought, the old way would have to do.

ONE OF THE sweetest memories from my childhood is the smell of freshly baked bread wafting through the porch door as I came into our yard from school. Mom learned to bake her bread at the Winstons. Too short to punch it down, she stood on a stool at the kitchen table, her fists pummelling. If the bread didn't turn out, she didn't get any supper, and after the others had eaten and she'd done the dishes, she had to start again, mixing the sugar, water and yeast, adding the liquid to the big bowl of flour, staying awake until the bread had risen, punching it down, letting it rise a second time, punching it down again, then putting it in the oven, and finally, the house in darkness, sliding its pans onto a wooden board to cool. She kept herself from sleeping by standing up, trying to balance on one leg, then the other. Even then, she dozed off like a horse on its feet, and the bread would have burned if something hadn't made her jerk awake. Mrs. Winston's yelling down the stairs, the tolling of the hours from the tall clock in the hallway, the image of her mother waking her up in the early morning to pick berries before the sun got too hot.

THE FAMILY took care of Mom at her house in Swift Current. We were a small group, just my brother, Barry, his wife, Linda, Patrick and me. We took turns coming from our homes, theirs in Cochrane, Alberta, and ours on Vancouver Island. Everything had happened fast. I'd arrived at her house on June 5, planning to drive her to her grandson's wedding in Calgary. On June 7 in the morning she had a colonoscopy, part of a regular checkup, which revealed a large tumour; by the afternoon we found out the cancer spotted her liver and had spread to her lymph nodes; the next morning she was under the scalpel. When the doctor told her he had to operate to remove part of her bowel, she said, "Oh, but we have a wedding to go to."

"We're not going to the wedding now, Mom," I said. It was the first time during her illness that her eyes had looked frightened, their blue blurred like startled water.

I was alone with her the week of her surgery. They wanted to take out the tumour, or at least part of it, to prevent the bowel from blocking completely. Pre-op, she told the nurses the last time she'd been in the hospital—the same hospital, as it turned out—was to give birth to me. Maybe because she'd been amazingly healthy all her life, even when she'd started losing weight and energy we thought she'd get better. Back in the winter she'd been diagnosed with diabetes; she'd be her old self soon, we believed, back to aqua exercises three times a week, meeting with her friends and single-handedly running a house and a big garden once her sugar levels got sorted out. No one, including her, had expected cancer. "At least I know what I'm going to die of," she said. "I always wondered about that."

Afraid I might never see her again, I sat with her before the operation, held her hand and choked out the words, "You are my shining light."

"And you're still my little girl," she said, "my skinny little girl who I couldn't get to eat." People would stop her on the street and ask why I was so big-eyed and thin. What was she feeding me? The truth was I'd eat almost nothing but bacon. Outside the porch on a wooden chair she'd leave pieces for me to snatch as I flew by like some wild child, not wanting to come in from playing. Who else could tell me that? Who but my mother held those small pieces of my childhood? Where would they go when she was gone?

It rained heavily the morning of her operation, as if the sky were the source of the tears pouring out of me. I went for a run for the hour and half it would take, my shoes pounding through puddles, and part of me, for her sake, wished she'd die on the table. No matter how the operation turned out, the liver cancer was devouring her from the inside out. There was no treatment, no cure, no lizard to stab and throw into the fire. Alone in her house in the shower, I started screaming as the spears of water hit my scalp and broke over me. Mom, mom, mom, mom! A yowl rose from my gut, my bowels, my womb, raw as a birth cry but with no hope in it, a maddened howl, a roar, the water a wailing wall shattering around me. Unsyllabled, thoughtless, the cry rose from the oldest cells in my body. I hadn't known grief could be so primal, so crude. The violence shook me. When it stopped, I fell to my knees in the shower, and the water called to the water in me; I wanted to melt, to run down the drain and under the city to the creek and then to the river thirty miles away. Mom, mom, mom, mom!

ON A HIGH frozen river, clouds piled like snow along the banks on either side, my mother and father are skating. The blades of their skates slice into the ice, their thighs strong and muscular. Arm in arm, they stride forwards, push, slide, push, slide, their faces flushed with cold and happiness. It is long before the drinking starts, long before my brother and I are born—and long after. That winter, the wisps of cloud I saw streaking the hard blue sky after the first night of freeze-up would be their joyous exhalations, their breaths intermingling as they glided down the glassy river somewhere past the moon.

THROUGHOUT MOM'S illness, Auntie Glad drove me crazy. She phoned at least five times a day. When I'd tell her Mom couldn't talk, she was lying down, Glad asked, "What's wrong with her? Sleeping at this hour!"

"She's sick," I said for the hundredth time. "She's not going to get better."

"Peggy's sick? I didn't know that."

I told you, Glad, I told you and told you and told you. Some days I had to repeat myself three or four times in one phone call because she wasn't wearing her hearing aid. I said the words I didn't want to say over and over again, my voice breaking with weariness and anger.

During one of her calls, I suggested she start thinking about moving to a place that could provide her with care. She wasn't able to keep track of things, and Mom wouldn't be able to help her any more.

"I'll die if I leave this house," she said.

"Well," I said, echoing my mother, "you have to die sometime."

I was ashamed to feel so little compassion. I just wanted her off my back, and I didn't want her bothering my mother, who refused to talk to her. "Tell her I'm asleep," Mom said when the phone rang.

"At least get a housecleaner," I told Glad. She had already fired two that year for pilfering things—a garden rake, a small roaster, her underwear. Mom had usually found the missing loot later, the panties in the cutlery drawer, for instance, but there was no convincing Glad that people weren't thieving.

She exploded, her voice suddenly hard and strong. "I'd rather be up to my ass in my own shit than let someone steal from me!"

I hung up the phone.

AT TIMES, I sensed impatience in the voices of my friends, slight yet noticeable as knots in a string. After all, as Mom said, I'd had a mother for a long time. Many people I knew had lost theirs decades earlier. Sixty million people die every year, half of them children under five. How could I explain that this impending death felt so huge it left me breathless, as if a rogue train was roaring out of the earth and bearing down on me, its round light blinding me to everything but sorrow, no one in the engine room, no warnings at the crossings, no one pulling on the brakes? Of the sixty million people who'd die that year, one of them would be my mother.

THE WINSTONS had two daughters. One of them was away at boarding school; the other, a few years older than my mother, did nothing to help around the house. The slave child spared her from the work most farm kids had to do. "She just watched me," Mom said.

My mother took meals by herself on a backless chair in the summer kitchen even when summer had passed. Besides baking bread, pulling weeds and doing dishes, the little girl my mother was cleaned the outhouse, limed the walls and scrubbed the floors. She cried on her first Christmas there, she told me, because they wouldn't let her go home. Angry that she wouldn't stop, they took away her present before she could open it.

The Winstons also held her back from grade 1—she didn't go until she was seven. No one had taught her how to count from one to ten or say the alphabet. No one had read stories to her or showed her pictures in a book.

Her first day in the one-room school, my mother raised her hand like everyone else when the teacher asked who could recite their ABCs. He picked her out. She sat in silence, kids turning in their desks to stare at her. Glad, who was eight grades ahead, walked to the front of the classroom and told the teacher her little sister had lied. Peggy didn't know anything.

ONE MORNING Mom looked at her ankles, which resembled the tiny bumps on poplar twigs where smaller twigs have broken off. She'd lost forty pounds in three months, and she was under five feet tall. "Poor little fellows," she said of her ankles. "They've disappeared, poor little things."

TO THE END of her life, my mother had a terrible fear of the storms that raged across the prairies. Mrs. Winston had always panicked when she heard thunder. In the parlour, she made Mom turn the handle of the phonograph so the music would block out the rumble and crash that shook the farmyard. She pushed back and forth in her rocker and yelled, "Faster, faster," the child's arm going numb, lightning flashing her small forlorn figure into the silver template of the sky while the needle bounced and screeched over the grooves of "Beautiful Dreamer," booms of thunder like a big hand slapping her head, making the bones jump in her inner ear.

ON THE PHONE from Cochrane my brother suggested I call Patrick and ask him to fly to Swift Current to be with me. Patrick had kept offering, but I'd been telling him to wait because I'd need him down the road. Barry said, "Sister, we're on the road." He was right.

When Patrick arrived we slept in Mom's room, in the bed she'd shared with my father. It should have felt stranger than it did, photos of Barry and me, our younger faces looking down at us from the wall. My mother had dragged herself like a wounded animal into the smaller of the two bedrooms, the darker one with her old sewing machine, the room I used to stay in. She'd begun to demand a simplicity of space, a nest, a cave. She said she'd never sleep in the other room again.

The first night on her old mattress Patrick had to wake me. I'd been shouting. In the nightmare I was searching through a many-roomed, three-storey house in a panic, looking for someone who needed me. I couldn't find her.

The next morning Patrick asked, "Who's Trudy?"

"Trudy?" I said.

"Do you know, Peg? That's the name Lorna was shouting in her sleep." Mom didn't know either, but suddenly I remembered. More than fifty years earlier a little girl my friend knew had wasted away in bed with leukemia. I had visited her once. Her name was Trudy.

"That's right," Mom said. "She was around six, and she died. You didn't know her well."

In the night I'd struggled to save a girl I hardly knew, my shouts echoing from her deathbed to my parents' room half a century away.

BEFORE THE OPERATION, a nurse had attached wires at various pulse points on my mother's body to check her heart rate. Her gown was open in the front. A wire went under each breast. I stared at the one nearest to me, fallen to the side. Since I was a baby, held to her nipple, I'd never looked so closely at my mother's naked breast. She was shorter than I was, we weren't the same shape, but our breasts had the same contour and colour. Her pink nipple could have been mine caught in a mirror. The awareness sank inside me like a stone, one with many sides to it, its light refracting. I wanted to think of it as a rose quartz. That came closest to the colour of our nipples, and it's the stone that heals the heart.

I STAYED with Auntie Glad on her and Uncle Rusty's farm only once. It had been my idea. I was around thirteen; I'd wanted to visit her because I was making a yellow-and-white-checked sundress with spaghetti straps for a Teen Town dance, and I couldn't get the straps right. Mom had tried to help me, but Glad was the better sewer. Besides her impeccably hand-stitched quilts, she fashioned coats and jackets with shiny linings, complicated lapels and smoothly rounded shoulders.

There was little warmth or affection in the farmhouse. Just cleanliness and hard work and the practicality of the day-to-day. An hour or so after my parents dropped me off, I got my period. It was the first time it had happened away from home, and I felt shy about it. I was mortified at having to ask my aunt what to do with the soiled pads. "Throw them in the burning barrel," she said, her tone suggesting I'd asked a stupid question. As if my period wasn't bad enough, I got a terrible nosebleed and dripped blood spots across the kitchen floor she'd waxed and polished just hours before. "Bleeding out of both ends," she said to Uncle Rusty when he came in from the barn. I don't think she meant to be unkind or crude. It was just her way.

I, like Mom, couldn't do anything right around Glad. When she asked me to make sandwiches out of the canned jellied chicken, I buttered the bread too thinly and she snapped at me. I'd heard all the stories of her cheapness and thought I was doing the right thing, saving her a teaspoonful of butter with each slice. My worst error was to correct her on how to make the straps on my sundress lie flat. I'd learned enough in home ec to know we needed some kind of binding. She'd never heard of such a thing. "If you're not going to listen you might as well go home," she said.

It was a relief to both of us when Dad picked me up at the end of my visit. Mom had warned me I wouldn't be happy at the farm. To avoid her saying "I told you so," with the assurance that made me furious, I claimed I'd had a great time and I would go back again. I wore the

166

dress to the dance that weekend, but the straps felt bumpy on my shoulders, and they wouldn't stay put. Mom was in bed when I got home. I slipped into my pyjamas, walked into the dark of the alley and threw the dress in the garbage can.

SOMETHING FUNNY happens to time when the world shrinks to a sickroom. Wind blows through the hours and shreds them into ragged strips. There's no definite beginning or end to one hour, two, three. In my mother's kitchen, meals weren't meals any more but vigils of waiting, as we watched each mouthful to see if she would chew and swallow. Our own eating seemed gluttonous, excessive. I wanted to push cake in my mouth with both hands and choke on thick gobs of sweetness. It was hard to shop for groceries. It was hard to cook something without onions or garlic or citrus or sugar or bite. Nights weren't eight or ten hours of sleep but a dark pane a brick had shattered into parts. Patrick and I listened to her shuffle from the bed to the bathroom—"Mom, are you okay?"—prayed she'd make it before her bowels exploded, the nerve damage from the operation shutting down her warning system. How many times that night? Four? Five? Would there be spoor to clean? She'd be worn out tomorrow. In the afternoon, who would come to visit, who would stop me in the street and ask me probing questions, who would phone, phone, phone? When was the ball game on? Would she want to watch it? Should she lie down now? Was it time to check her sugar level? Write down the number, throw out the cotton batten with the spot of blood, count out the pills, count out her years and years, and soon the afternoon was over. Should we wake her to eat? There was no pain yet; we prayed there never would be. How long, how long, how long, the invisible clock kept ticking, the two hands meeting somewhere out of sight. "I'm ready to go," she said. "Time. It's time."

On my wrist I wore my father's watch, an old one I'd found in a kitchen drawer at Mom's a few years after he died. It wasn't his last watch—that was a gold-banded Seiko Mom had bought him for his seventieth birthday. It was the kind a high school teacher would wear, or a businessman, or a lawyer. Even in his final days, when he didn't know the day of the week or the month, he'd ask my mother for the exact time and then move the hands to get the numbers right.

The watch I found was much older. He'd worn it when he was in his forties and working in the oil fields. It had a luminous blue face and a wide leather band still dark on the underside from his sweat, and it was one of the earliest automatics. It depended on the movement of your arm to keep it going. If you took it off, it slowed and eventually stopped. With new holes punched in the strap so it would fit me, the watch felt heavy and significant above my left hand, as if the ghost of my father's fingers encircled my wrist. I removed it at night and placed it on the bedside table. In the mornings it was always slow, about five minutes. It gave me the kind of time I could understand, one that needed my body in all its strength to power its wheels now that my father lay still.

OUT OF A DEMEROL sleep my mother sat straight up in her hospital bed, terror in her eyes. "There's a big hole in front of me. Lorna, fill it, start filling it." Later she tried to send me home. "I don't understand why you're here," she said. "You should be with Patrick."

On one of her good days back at home, though she hadn't been on her feet for over a week, she walked into her backyard, checked out the rows of plants with her sharp gardener's eye, walked to one particular potato plant and pulled the top. The bounty underneath filled the bowl she used for baking bread. Linda took a picture, the bowl larger than Mom's lap. That night for supper, standing at the stove with one hand on the counter to hold her up, she boiled potatoes and fried fish for Barry and Linda. Later in the week, when they had gone and it was my turn to care for her, she fried some for me, too—so I wouldn't think my brother was her favourite, she told me, a smile on her face. With shaky hands, before she let me eat, she tried to pick out the bones as she had when I was a child, afraid one would catch in my throat and choke me. No one has ever loved me better.

THE CITY WHERE I grew up, where Mom had lived for almost seventy years, had hired an ad agency from Calgary to update its image. The councillors voted to change the city's original slogan, "Swift Current, the Frontier City," to "Swift Current, Where Life Makes Sense." I wanted to write the local paper and rage. How could they claim that life made sense anywhere, especially there, especially then?

The slogan proclaimed its simple-minded self-satisfaction on the sign that greeted you when you arrived in town. It was printed on banners on the streets; it appeared on gas and water bills. Hundreds of great philosophers and writers had come to the opposite conclusion, but in Swift Current you could figure things out—why there was sadness and cheating and inequity and wife-beating and racism. Why most of the wildflowers and songbirds from my childhood had disappeared. Why my friend's eleven- and twelve-year-old sons had died in a car accident, why the local history teacher had hanged herself, why the hockey team had hired a pedophile for a coach. It all made sense, by gosh, in my hometown, where my heart was ripping out of my chest like a blood-soaked bird.

ON THE PHONE Auntie Glad demanded to talk to Mom. "Wake her up, wake her up. They're coming to get me."

"Who?"

"I don't know. I think it's the gypsies."

"Do you want to go?" I asked.

"I don't know. I like their bracelets. I like their gold teeth, but they look at you funny—like a horse does. They can't look at you with both eyes at once."

MOM DIDN'T want get out of bed. I curled up beside her, laid my hand on her bony forehead. Her face had lost its roundness; her temples were shadowed, as if a printer's thumb blue with ink had pressed there. Before a baby's eyebrows appear, there are two delicate ridges above the eyes where the soft hair will grow in. They were apparent on Mom now. It was as if her body was set on rewind, running backwards to an earlier time.

"Do you know how to find Dad?" she said in the perpetual dusk of the room. I didn't know what she was asking. Did I know where he was in the afterworld she believed in? Had God built for her a mansion with many rooms? Was her husband waiting for her in one of them, or was her heaven a countryside, a series of farms and villages, different roads to navigate, the dead dogs barking?

She was worried we wouldn't find the spring that fed into the alkali lake on her parents' farm where we'd scattered Dad's ashes. The previous July she and I had driven out there and couldn't locate it, maybe because Uncle Lyn, who now owned the land, hadn't cut the grass for bales, and the old cow path was grown over.

"I think it was the mosquitoes, Mom. We didn't walk far enough because of the mosquitoes. But we'll find it, because the grass will be greener near the spring, won't it? And there's that big stone." Against her pillow, her face was jaundiced. I'd packed away the yellow blouses and T-shirts from her closet. They didn't look good on her anymore.

"Do you want things to happen as you told me, Mom? Just the family and the lake? All those friends who've been phoning, they're going to want a way to say goodbye."

"Don't you dare give me a funeral," she said, the toughness in her voice a warning signal familiar from my childhood. "I don't want a funeral. Just toss my ashes on the water. I've always loved the lake."

"Soon you'll be there forever, Mom."

"Swimming with the ducks," she said. "And I'll have a new bathing suit. Or maybe I'll go skinny-dipping now that I'm so skinny."

"And that water," I said, "that awful alkali water will never let you drown."

I'd learned it was possible to cry and laugh at the same time, to cry and talk at the same time, to cry and cry though you thought the well of tears was empty. An unseen endless spring kept flowing in and out of me. My mother, however, had yet to cry. It was if she had dried up inside. Was that one of the things that let me know how close she was to dying? The Mycenaean Greeks called the dead "the thirsty" and their place "the dry country." It would be tragic if after all the years of living in parched Saskatchewan my mother were to spend eternity in a sere country of wind and dust.

For her sake, I hoped eternity was no more than a person's happiest experience, best imaginings, deepest longings: a lake that tastes bitter on the tongue; a long frozen river a man and woman glide down, arm in arm, among the stars; a clear sky higher than all other skies where no storms gather.

ONE OF THE WORST things Mom did as a kid was to accept her older brother Mac's dare to walk around the rim of the horse trough. She fell in, her siblings laughing, but when Grandpa came with his team from the fields, the horses wouldn't drink. Water was scarce, and to fill the trough took several trips to the pump with a pail. "Boy, was Grandpa mad," she said. She didn't remember what he did to her, but she remembered it was Glad who told.

THERE WOULD be no family for me when Mom was gone except my brother and my beloved, Patrick, nine years my senior. My breath stopped when I thought of Patrick going first.

Barry had left home when I was eleven, and since then, we'd rarely been in touch. I'd thought his love was like hard candies in his pocket; once they'd been slipped to those closest to him—his wife and children—there was nothing left. The weeks after Mom fell ill were different. He was a devoted brother and son. When we weren't in Swift Current together, we were on the phone every day, wondering if we were doing the right thing and what should happen next. I had a new appreciation of him, new insight into the sensitivity he hid behind gruffness and firm action, habits from his years as a hockey player and then a captain in the air force and a helicopter rescue pilot. When we greeted each other we hugged and kissed, and on the phone he sometimes called me "dear." Would he be lost to me again, I wondered, after Mom was gone?

We agreed we'd take care of her in her house for as long as we could. We wouldn't dump her in one of those terrible nursing homes where the old and demented shout and drool. That was no place for our mother.

WHEN DAD LAY DYING, he told Mom he'd dreamed he'd gone to heaven. "Did you meet anyone you know?" she asked. "No," he said. He'd only made it halfway there.

173

SINCE I'D MOVED to the coast fifteen years earlier, every Mother's Day, which fell around Mom's birthday, I'd fly to visit. We'd drive my rental car to the nursery by the creek and buy her rose bushes for her front bed. You'd think we'd have filled it up in that time, but the bed took up half the yard, and many roses didn't make it through the winter. Usually I'd buy her three each spring, choosing by colour. She had several pinks, a mauve like the underside of a dove's breast, a pale peach, a yellow the shade of a mango's skin, four reds, a cream like the tasty pout that rose to the top of the old milk bottles in winter. A sure sign of her illness was that she'd let her rose garden go that year. It bristled with sow thistles and a sticky, nettle-like vine that strangled the stems and buds.

Mom told me not to bother, but I spent hours weeding and deadheading. A lassitude had fallen over the garden, many of the branches bending to the ground as if they'd lost the will to stand upright. It wasn't blossoms that were weighing them down. I couldn't figure it out. One red rose had gone wild, shooting out a thin, pulsing brightness on leggy branches. Its scent rode the heat waves and washed over me. Mom insisted I cut it down; then the tea rose that had been grafted might come back. On other bushes the buds were tight and dry. They seemed stopped in time and wouldn't open. Was something eating them from the inside, too? I lacked my mother's wisdom and her touch. I couldn't save them, yet I couldn't give up. I hacked and weeded and tore, my hands grabbing where I shouldn't have grabbed and holding on.

"WHEN I SEE your dad again," Mom said, "we're going to go dancing."

"Dancing? A few weeks ago, you said you were going to go skating."

"I know," she said, "but who can tell what season it will be up there? Maybe it won't be cold enough for ice."

MOM DECIDED in her implacable way that she wanted to go into a nursing home. A space would be available two days thence. Over the phone, Patrick tried to help me understand. "She wants care with compassion, not care with love," he told me. There was no stopping her. I was afraid she was doing it because she'd become a "bother," something she swore she'd never be.

"You kids have your normal lives to lead," she said.

Nothing's normal, Mom, I thought, not anymore.

She had me confirm the booking and phone the ambulance. She'd be going to the town of Leader, an hour and a half away on the worst road in the province.

"I've never ridden in an ambulance before," she said, joy in her voice. She was like a kid going to the circus, like a country cousin anticipating the train that would take her to the city. Why was I sad when she was ecstatic? What was it I wasn't getting? Would I ever arrive before she'd left where she'd already been? No trace of her but a pair of abandoned shoes.

I'D ALWAYS liked the idea of a body's energy returning to the great mass of energy that makes up the world, its spirit and its matter. If I became the force that drove the worm through the rosebud, if I greened a blade of prairie grass—I could live and die with that. Now, though, I wanted my mother to remain intact. I wanted her to be up there looking down at me. I didn't want to lose her to the grass, the trees, the beetles, the crickets. I wouldn't be satisfied with her hair blowing from the mouths of the crocuses in the spring, her stubbornness and persistence driving the wind that pushed me along the road. What had sounded earth-affirming no longer comforted me. "Mom," I said, "you'd better drop a pebble on my head now and then when I'm being stupid, just to show me you're there."

She grinned a sweet grin that didn't reach her eyes any more. They'd become flat, like the circle of water inside a well no wind or light could reach. "You better watch out! One day it will be a big stone."

WHEN MOM went to the nursing home, she'd be leaving her house forever. They'd told her to bring her favourite chair, her television and anything else that would make her feel at home. Linda and I packed her summer clothes and a quilt. In her bedroom hung the old family photos of her wedding and of my brother and me. I asked her which pictures she wanted us to tuck into her suitcase. "I don't want any of them," she said. "I'm done with all that."

When the ambulance arrived, she met the two attendants on the verandah and walked with them down the four front steps to the stretcher. Not once, in her journey away from what she had known and loved for almost thirty years, did she look back.

THE DAY before Mom was to leave, I asked her about Glad. "Do you want to phone and tell her you're going?"

"No. You go over and let her know. I don't want to talk to her."

I walked into Glad's house without knocking, because I knew she wouldn't hear. I sat beside her on the couch and turned off the TV. The couch was piled with newspapers, a Kleenex box, ends of wool balls, cards from her birthday a month earlier, and a half-eaten ham sandwich on brown bread. "Auntie Glad," I said, "Mom is leaving her house tomorrow and going into a home. She won't be back."

"I didn't know she was sick," Glad said.

"I know you're confused, but I've been telling you for weeks about the cancer and that she's not getting better."

"You never know," Glad said, "you never know what's going to happen, do you? I suppose I'll go soon too."

She was even shorter than Mom, the widow's hump in her back hunching her shoulders. Sitting beside her, I could see the top of her head where her hair was thinning. Her scalp shone a pale pink. We were both having trouble talking. Her voice was a thousand years old.

I held her hand. "I was so happy," she said, "when I found out I had a little sister. I'd had two brothers, you know, and then I had a little sister. I took care of her. Should I go over and say goodbye? I don't know if I can do it."

"It's okay," I said. "She's sleeping, and we're leaving early tomorrow, there won't be time. I don't want anything to upset her."

I took my hand from hers and placed hers in her lap. "Do you understand," I asked, "do you understand what

I've just told you? She doesn't have much time left. And she's leaving her house for good tomorrow. She's going to a home."

"Yes," she said. "It's so sad, isn't it, it's so sad."

I turned the TV on again and asked if the volume was okay. Our conversation had taken only a few minutes: the commercials were still on. I walked from her house and across the street to Mom's. I was walking across an entire continent, across years of bitterness and anger and love. No maps, no easy passage. I wanted to lie in the middle of the road and never move again.

WHILE WE WAITED for the ambulance, I'd told Mom what Glad had said about wanting a sister. My mother's eyes brightened with tears, the first I'd seen, but they didn't spill over. "This was the best way for us to say goodbye," she said. "I don't want to see her."

IT WASN'T ONLY the roses that defeated us that summer. In the back garden stretched rows and rows of peas and potatoes and beans. Barry and Linda spent two days digging and picking and shelling, until Barry's back gave out. Linda said she'd never been so dirty in her life. They left the rest for me and Patrick. Our troubles amused Mom in the nursing home. She couldn't believe we were so useless, so weak.

And what would we do with pails and pails of vegetables? None of us, including the grandchildren, had a basement cold room like she did. We didn't eat that many potatoes anymore. Their fate concerned her more than the roses. There was too much Welsh and Irish in our family history, too much poverty, to leave them. The flowers could die, even from neglect, but you didn't let potatoes rot in the ground or peas harden on the vines. If there had been a magical way to call the grackles down, I'd have done it. Mom always flew small flags along the rows of peas to scare them off. I wanted the opposite, a flirtatious flutter. And where were the bad kids who raided gardens like we used to do, just for the danger of it? How had this old woman picked and shelled and dug and dug and dug until this final summer of her life?

A FEW DAYS after we'd settled Mom in the nursing home, Linda took a deserved break. I drove alone to Leader. Barry was in Cochrane and would join us soon. Though only a chair and a small television were missing, the house felt hollowed out and sadly animate, as if it knew the tough, beloved spirit that was my mother would not grace its rooms again.

In the bathroom, the door locked, Linda lowered herself into the full, deep tub. She heard the back door open, and then footsteps up the stairs and through the kitchen. "Peggy," an old woman's voice called again and again. "Peggy, where are you?" Glad wandered through the house, calling and calling. Linda sat still and silent in the cooling water. "Peggy, are you home?"

not waving but
drowning

WHEN I SAW my mother again, it wasn't where I'd expected. Not in the rose bed in the front yard of her small house. Maybe she knew better than to go there; a year after her death, weeds towered above the bushes I could barely see. The new owners weren't tending them. The whole house looked shabby, as it had never looked before.

My brother had rototilled the vegetable garden before he locked up the house the previous September. Now it was the second week of July, but as I drove down the alley past the backyard, I saw only thistles pushing meanly from the soil. I knew instantly Mom wasn't there, and I felt strangely calm about the house's slide into neglect. It really didn't matter. The house was shaping itself not around my mother but around the people who lived there now. Instead of the garden, the young couple, newly married, had different things on their minds.

I hoped to see my mother at the new house on the coast Patrick and I moved into four months after she died. We'd used the small amount of money that was my inheritance to upgrade to a place on a quieter street with more light. I wanted to show her the garden, fashioned out of moss and water and stones, and the guest room, furnished with her dresser with its round mirror and her bed with the tulip quilt Auntie Glad had made and sold to her for more than it was worth. "You'd think she could have given it to me," Mom said, "after all I've done for her."

There was a park across the road from our new house, with a trail leading to the ocean. I wanted to walk with her through the trees to the shore. We could wade in together, me in rubber shoes, her barefoot; surely the stones could no longer hurt her feet. In the nursing home, a couple of weeks before the end, she'd told me one morning that her feet had died in the night. "What do you mean?" I asked. "Are they numb? Did you feel pins and needles?"

No, she said. She had just woken up and known her feet had gone on ahead. They were already dancing. She was so happy. "Soon I'll join them," she said.

EVERY JULY for the past twenty-five years, I've spent two weeks at a monastery an hour out of Saskatoon. It turns into a college come fall, but it's also a year-round working farm. It's a place for me to write and to visit the chicken sheds and barns, to talk to the horses behind the fence and to touch the velvet of their mouths if they'll let me.

The year I turned fifty, I was diagnosed with melanoma. On the side of my right foot a freckle had grown to twice its size. The surgeon cut it out and stitched on a piece of skin grafted from my upper thigh. Before I learned that I had to avoid the sun, I used to walk past the tall school building at the abbey to the running track and sit on the highest level of the bleachers where there wasn't a lick of shade.

Surrounded by a curve of spruce, the track hasn't been used in years. For some reason it comforts me to see it so solidly there, the grass it circles overgrown with short white clover, the blossoms exactly the size and shape of the plastic beads we wore as kids. The beads popped together and pulled apart so you could make a necklace or bracelet of whatever length you wanted. That's where I saw my mother, at the track, sitting on the top bench, her sturdy legs brown below her shorts, the pair she had pinned at the waist so she could wear them those last weeks in the home. She had a top to match.

I had driven her to the Wal-Mart on the edge of Swift Current to buy the material, a thin, cheap cotton blazing with red flowers. Her hems were always lumpy, but you didn't notice the imperfections once she pulled on her homemade outfits. She looked so good in them, though nothing she sewed for me fit right. She didn't have the patience to finish things properly.

People respect the need for solitude at the monastery. Normally, I wouldn't have spoken to someone on the bleachers. But there was something about the way the person sat, the shortness of her legs and her rounded shoulders, that made me go nearer.

"Finally," my mother said, then grinned. "I didn't know you were such a dawdler."

I climbed to the top and sat beside her, as if our meeting had been pre-arranged. "You didn't expect to see me here, did you?" she said. I dug my elbows into my ribs to keep from crying. That's all she'd seen me do the last two months of her life. Every word I'd spoken was soggy then, and barely understandable.

"You always surprise me," I said to my mother. I put my hand on her bare arm. Her skin was warm, as if she'd spent all day in her garden, her smell familiar, a mix of dust and sun and the good sweat of outdoor labour. I was afraid to say anything else in case she'd disappear.

A crow from one of the spruce trees started cawing. "At home we would've shot him," she said. "For stealing robins' eggs. I wish your dad had taught me how to use a gun."

"I didn't know you'd be thinking of killing things, Mom. I mean, in the place you went to."

"You have *no* idea," she said. "And I'm not here to tell you. I'm here for you to see the runner." She pointed to the far end of the track.

I peered at the track and past it, into the row of spruce lined up like monks in evergreen cowls, but I couldn't see a runner. Just the crow on top of one of the trees, the branch dipping with his weight, and smaller birds I couldn't make out diving around him. From where we sat we could hear the highway, the whoosh of cars and trucks going somewhere fast. The air carried the sound so clearly you could hear the tires strike a patch where the pavement had heaved in the winter or worn thin.

"I can't see anything, Mom."

"You never could see what was right in front of your nose," she said, patting me on the knee. "You were always looking for something else."

"Do *you* see a runner?"

"You writers are supposed to be so smart!" There was mischief in her voice, as if she wanted to get a rise out of me. "You know one thing that happens? The dead get their real teeth back." She opened her mouth. "See, these aren't false any more, they're real. Oh, there he goes, another lap."

"Mom," I said, "I don't get it." Dragonflies bucked in the air like small winged ponies trying to toss the sun off their backs. They hunted in posses, and I felt good sitting in their midst as they devoured mosquitoes.

Mom looked at me the way she used to when I'd done something that pleased her, when I was the apple of her eye. "I'm really here to tell you to wear a hat."

"You've come just to tell me that?"

"Yes," she said, the wind in the spruce trees picking up. I thought that might be a signal for her to vanish; she never liked the wind. I wanted to say, Mom, don't go, but I didn't. I knew how ready she'd been to leave the world.

"Okay," she said, "one more thing. I'm glad you took the dresser. The first time you saw your face, almost sixty years ago, was in that mirror. I held you up and introduced you to yourself. Baby, I said, this is you. Think of that and maybe you won't feel so sad." She pointed again at the track. "There he goes," she said.

My god, I could see him! A teenage boy in a red baseball cap running in the sunny half, his thighs and arms pumping. He wasn't a ghost. He had the grace of the living and the young. In fact, I'd seen him yesterday in the Muenster post office picking up a parcel from the woman behind the counter. He told her he was going to school that fall to finish the high school classes he'd missed. He wanted to go into criminal justice and maybe become a Mountie.

The boy stopped in front of us, bent over, catching his breath. The sun burned behind him. "I don't seem to get any faster," he said. When he straightened, I could see he wasn't the teenager who wanted to be a Mountie after all, but the middle-aged man who helped with the haying on the abbey. He lived in a trailer near the big barn. Just as I was wondering if he could see my mother, I sensed an emptiness beside me.

She was gone, and in the time it took to look at where she'd been, the runner was halfway down the track. Why had she wanted me to see him? Was it to remind me life goes fast? It's as short as a run around a track, a boy turning into a man the age of his father, just like that? My mother had never talked in symbols. About my poems, she used to ask, why don't you just say what you mean? Surely I was missing something.

I let the wind blow over me and through my hair. That was one of the reasons I didn't wear a hat; the wind blew my stale thoughts away. The surface of the track was pocked like the dips in an old bathing cap. Rain had hammered the earth two nights before, the sheet lightning so bright and frequent it was as if the sky were taking pictures with a flash.

The birds that had been dive-bombing the crow were gone. The crow was gone. When I tipped my head, the sky held the reflection of my face, though I couldn't see it, like in the bevelled circular mirror of my mother's dresser. Baby, she had said almost sixty years ago, this is you.

I SAW HER again two weeks later. It was my last day at the abbey, and I was walking the grid in the early morning. I stared at the wheat field to the east, trying to measure how much of it had turned to gold. It had been green when I arrived. At first I thought it was a trick of the light, but in the middle of the field someone seemed to be waving. It could only be my mother, I thought. No one else would be in the middle of a wheat field in the middle of nowhere.

She and I were no strangers to walking. How often the two of us would trudge home from somewhere downtown through blinding snow. Maybe that's why she thought it wouldn't bother me to plow halfway down a wheat field. I was anxious that the farmer would catch me and bawl me out. Anyone, even people born in cities, knew you didn't do that. You didn't tread through perfectly good wheat, flattening a row the combine couldn't pick up. My mother had been a farm kid. I wondered why she'd chosen this spot to turn up again. If it had been her father's field, she'd have been punished.

"Wonderful here, isn't it?" she said. "You almost disappear."

She was right. If she hadn't raised her arms and waved she would have been invisible. A few inches taller, I could barely see above the ripe seed heads. She might have been light enough for me to hoist on my shoulders, but I didn't try. She stood on a small flattened circle in the field, but there was no wheat trodden down, no path leading to her. You would have sworn a dozen gophers had stampeded to where I stood. I felt hot and sticky, the sun branding the back of my neck. "Where's your hat?" she asked. I showed her the hood on my T-shirt. "I pull it up when the sun's out," I said. I demonstrated how it covered my head.

"If you're going to do something halfway, don't do it at all," she said, familiar words from my childhood. Then, "Don't worry, I won't nag. You'll only get stubborn and not listen."

"Mom, are you going to disappear like last time, with no warning?" Mosquitoes were starting to find me, buzzing and diving for my skin. I slapped my arm, then my shoulder, the tops of my hands. Though her arms and legs were bare—she wore the same outfit as before but in a different material, this one a pale blue denim—the mosquitoes didn't bother her. I didn't want to think about that.

"There was something I'd forgotten to ask," she said. "How is he?"

"Barry's fine," I said. "I saw him a month ago."

"No, not your brother. I know how *he* is. I mean Dr. Phil."

Dr. Phil? I didn't remember Mom being so intimate with any of the doctors at the Swift Current hospital or the care home in Leader. It had always been Dr. and then some long last name we found difficult to pronounce: once it was Pakistani, once Nigerian, once Sri Lankan. To the first doctor, the internist whose skin was the colour of mahogany, she'd said, "Your shirt is so white. Your wife must take good care of you." It had made me cringe.

"Dr. *Phil,* you silly, on TV. You know who I mean."

Dr. Phil was one of the daily programs I'd watched with her when I was home on a visit. The other was *Regis and Kelly* from New York. She didn't miss either show except on the days they conflicted with her aqua exercises. I never watched them on my own. It was one of the things we did together to pass the time. "Why do you want to know about Dr. Phil?" I asked.

"There's something you need to hear from him," she said.

I couldn't imagine what that would be. I found Dr. Phil a self-righteous bully. And I had his message down pat after watching only a few programs with her: you have a choice in this life, you don't have to accept someone else's bad behaviour and you must own up to your own. Didn't I know that already? After all these years was I still blaming my regrets and flaws on my parents?

"Mom, you've come all the way from wherever you are to tell me to watch Dr. Phil? There's so much I want you to tell me." She started to blur, the edges of her watery, like heat waves rising from asphalt on the highway. "Okay, okay, don't go! I'm sorry. I'll watch Dr. Phil."

"Anyway, I'm not supposed to tell you much. I promised," she said.

Promised? Promised who? I didn't ask. On all sides the wheat was so lush and thick you couldn't see past it; it was a jungle of stalk after golden stalk you'd need machetes to break through. I could see the sky only when I tipped my head, but my hearing seemed sharper, finely tuned like a cat's. Whispers rippled through the field. It was just the wind, I said to myself, the wind catching up on gossip with the ripening grasses.

"Mom, what's it like there? Do you see Dad? Is it like being back on the farm?"

"There ain't no raisins in my rice pudding," she said, looking right at me. Her eyes were the clear, almost indigo blue I'd found so beautiful before they'd clouded over in the last weeks of her life.

"That sounds like the start of a blues song, Mom."

"Well, you sing it, sweetie pie. I don't have a voice."

"What do you mean? You're talking to me now." A tractor started up in the distance. It was the sound a ruffed grouse makes when he's mating, but this was the wrong season for that. I tried another tack. "Where you are—are you dancing?"

"How could you not dance with the angels?" she said, grinning. "On the end of a hatpin. A pearl one, the smoothest, whitest floor you could ever glide across. Like a sheet of ice. Imagine that!"

"Mom," I said, "get serious." She'd never talked like this before. "Are you happy? What's it like? Is Dad there with you?"

"What's the name of this wheat?" she asked. "I used to know that when I was young. Now it's all just wheat, wheat, wheat. Let me tell you, when you're dead, what you've forgotten doesn't come back. Keep remembering," she said. "You don't get another chance." She rubbed her eyes, as if she were tired. "I cry a lot now, can you believe that? All the tears the dead don't shed on earth, they do after. I don't know why. I should've cried when I saw you meet the Queen. What was it she said to you again when she shook your hand?"

A year before her death I'd recited a poem at the gala performance for the Queen during Saskatchewan's centennial. It was at the command of the lieutenant governor, who was my childhood friend Lynda. Sometimes, on a television news clip, Mom and I would catch a glimpse of her handing out medals or giving a speech. "Didn't she turn out wonderful?" my mother always said. "She looks so tall and elegant."

Once Lynda had finished high school, with her baby and a new husband, she went on to university in Saskatoon. She'd become a specialist on learning disabilities, later a psychologist, then leader of the Saskatchewan Liberal Party. Now she was lieutenant governor of the province.

After the gala's curtain call, the performers had lined up on stage. The Queen and Prince Philip walked through the line, pausing before a couple of us to say a word or two. My mother had been in the audience. The evening, May 19, had coincided with her eighty-seventh birthday.

"She said I was a great duster."

Mom laughed, remembering my childhood fantasy. Her laugh was robust, not the nervous one that used to punctuate much of what she said, funny or not. The hardest I'd ever heard her laugh was the day she had told Patrick and me about putting Dad's hearing aid through the wash by mistake. Since then, he'd complained about it making a racket. It had screeched so much he didn't want to wear it. "I haven't told him," she'd said. "He'd be so disgusted with me." She'd laughed so outrageously that tears had run down her face and her belly jiggled.

"C'mon now," she said. "Tell me about the Queen."

"She said wasn't it wonderful that Lynda and I had been friends since we were children." Lynda, who'd sat beside the Queen during the gala, must have told her about us growing up together.

"Lynda was so much bigger than you," Mom said. "She used to twirl you around and let you drop as if you didn't have any bones. I was afraid you'd get hurt."

"Remember when she got mad at you," I said—neither Lynda nor I could remember why—"and threw dirt on the sheets you'd just hung on the line? She still feels guilty about that."

Clouds gathered on the horizon and began dragging their shadows over the far end of the field. They glided towards us like barges carrying a heavy freight. Everyone would be praying their cargo was rain.

"Mom," I said, "I have so many questions I wish I'd asked you."

"That's the way it goes," she said.

"Not even big ones, but little things. Like what year did Dad work at the horse plant, and what did he do there? Did he kill horses?"

"So many things I wanted to ask my own mother," she said. "Most of them amounted to nothing—recipes, how to sew in a zipper so it wouldn't look puckery, the words to the song she used to sing when she was ironing with that old flat iron that burnt your hand so easily. The most important one I couldn't ask: why she didn't love me?"

"Mom, are you coming back? Can we talk some more?"

A silence fell between us. It was like the one I'd felt every Sunday morning since her death, when I wanted to pick up the phone and punch in our old number, the one I'd memorized as a kid before I could even dial. I could hear the phone ringing and ringing in the house that existed now only in my mind. She wasn't there to answer. But still

I'd think: she must be out in the garden in her old shoes; she must be walking to the credit union to pay her bills or to the post office with a letter, my address in her familiar handwriting on the envelope. If it was a week before my birthday, there'd be $50 inside it, money she'd saved from her pension. The phone kept ringing. Surely someone would answer if I didn't hang up.

"Just one question, Mom. Please, before you go. Will I get to be with you in heaven when I die?"

"What makes you think I know about heaven?" she said.

And with that, she was gone. I stood at the end of the path I'd made to my mother, the wheat field spinning its gold around me. I raised my arms above my head and gestured wildly, but no one that I could see was waving back.

first cause: story

OVER WHIST and gin rummy, during chicken plucking
and berry picking, after baseball games in the pasture
among cow pies, the stories come as talk and chatter. Your
parents were only children during the Dirty Thirties, but
you could swear you lived through that time with them.
"You'll never know what it was like," your mother says, but
you do, you do. Her words recast the light, spin the earth
into dust the wind never stops turning over and over in
its restless hands.

Not yet born, invisible, you stand beside your mother
as she slips into the flour-sack pyjamas her mother stitched
by hand. You feel the coarseness of the cotton on your
skin. You squish your toes inside the shoes that never fit.
At Christmas, you breathe in the rare citrus smell of the
orange that must be shared among seven children, the
youngest sister getting a whole one to herself because she
was ill as a baby and has curly hair. By the barn, you watch
your grandfather hitch his horses to the wagon and drive
to town to wait in line for the train from the East. He hates
being there, but he doesn't let it show. He uses the time to
visit with his neighbours, though he keeps his back straight
and looks down the tracks with blue eyes leached a paler
blue by the sky's cloudless stare.

The train at last arrives with apples and hay from Ontario, smoked cod from Newfoundland, turnips that taste sweet—the few grown at home are bitter—clothes that carry the smell and grime of those who've outgrown them. Sometimes, mixed in with the fraying wool sweaters and pants with see-through knees, there are books with brittle yellow pages. To your delight, a few have pages missing. You claim one as your own, fill in where the story pauses before it picks up again. You change the setting, using the names of your birthplace. You call up the sere images you've inherited as you have your freckled skin and your mother's fretting, her capacity for worry and hard work. This ache, this country of wind and dust and sky, is your starting point, the way you understand yourself, the place you return to when there's nowhere else to go. It is the pared-down language of your blood and bones.

Your words go deeper, darkened by drought's long shadow. It sweeps across the fields and towns and everything that lives here, even in the cities with their glass and concrete and watered greens. Wherever you go, you speak with the earth on your tongue, in the accent passed down for generations. It's a lengthening of vowels, a dusty drawl thin enough to be carried some distance by the wind.

acknowledgements

MY DEEPEST APPRECIATION goes to Patrick Lane, for his love and belief in me. I also want to thank Rob Sanders, who encouraged me to write this book, and Barbara Pulling, who did more than her usual inspired line-by-line editing. She helped me find the shape of the book and gave me the perspective I needed to complete it. There is no editor like her. My thanks also go to the Swift Current Museum for assisting me with my research. Finally, my thanks to the University of Victoria for its support of my research and to the Saskatchewan Writers/ Artists Colony at St. Peter's Abbey, where I wrote the early drafts of this book. To my brother, Barry, to Ona and to Lynda, apologies for any factual errors I might have made, and a warm thank you for letting me tell our stories and use your real names. In several other cases, I have changed people's names.

The book's epigraph comes from *Apology for Absence: Selected Poems 1962–1992* by John Newlove (Porcupine's Quill, 1993). John Berger's *Here Is Where We Meet* (Blooms-bury, 2005) inspired the last chapter. Its title, "Not Waving but Drowning," comes from Stevie Smith; it is the title of her poetry collection published in 1957 by Andre Deutsch.

The quote from the Talmud, along with the description of the Mycenaean Greek afterlife and their name for the dead referred to in "My Mother for a Long Time," comes from Annie Dillard's *For the Time Being* (Vintage, 2000).

Earlier versions of some of these stories appeared in *Geist, Focus, Perfectly Secret: The Hidden Lives of Seven Teen Girls, My Wedding Dress, Dropped Threads* and *Dropped Threads 3*.

GARTH MARTENS

LORNA CROZIER, one of Canada's most celebrated poets, has published over fifteen books, edited several anthologies and received numerous awards, including the Governor General's Award for *Inventing the Hawk.* She lives in Saanich, British Columbia. *www.lornacrozier.ca*